Love & Life

A Poetic Journey Back to Truth

ABI WOLDEAB

Andrews McMeel
PUBLISHING®

The authorised representative in the EEA is Simon and Schuster Netherlands BV, Herculesplein 96 3584 AA Utrecht, Netherlands. (info@simonandschuster.nl)

Andrews McMeel Publishing
a division of Andrews McMeel Universal
1130 Walnut Street, Kansas City, Missouri 64106

www.andrewsmcmeel.com

26 27 28 29 30 TEN 10 9 8 7 6 5 4 3 2 1

ISBN: 979-8-8816-0278-9

Library of Congress Control Number: On file

Editor: Danys Mares
Art Directors: Tiffany Meairs and Brittany Lee
Production Editor: Elizabeth A. Garcia
Production Manager: Julie Skalla

Cover art and illustrations by Serena Woldeab

Love & life

Love is like recycled rain:
It never runs out.

It pours into one
that pours into another
that pours back into
the one.

Its source is infinite
and forever flowing.

And so with life to live,
there is always
love to give.

Contents

LOVE

The push you need to start

What would life look like
if we took every chance we had?
What would life look like
if we weren't afraid
to make the big moves
and try something new?

I wonder
if all we need is some gratitude.
For all we have
and all we've been through.

Maybe it's in letting go
of the perspective we have
and the fears that we grab.
Releasing control
to discover our true role,
allowing life to play out
with time and patience,
with thanks
and a little less fear
for what is to come.

Then maybe,
with a little more faith,
we'll be blessed
with the grace
to finish our own race.

Enough

I might not have everything,
but I have what I need.

I might not have everything,
but I have hope in my heart, so I can dream.

I might not have everything,
but I have breath in my lungs,
so I can speak.

I might not have everything,
but I have faith in my soul, so I am free.

I might not have everything,
but I have what I need.

Climb

I think back on my greatest heartbreaks—
on the betrayal and pain
that I thought I would never work through.
I look back on those days,
and all I have to say is
thank you.

Thank you for breaking my heart so bad
that I had no one to turn to but God.

Thank you for leaving me in the dirt,
because I had to learn my worth.
I had to learn that, whether you said it or not,
whether you showed it or not,
my value remained.
Regardless of how you saw me,
regardless of how you treated me,
my worth remains.

Thank you for showing me
that I am so much more than I can see,
that my heart can be misleading,
and these feelings?
These feelings are fleeting.

Thank you for showing me
that my rock bottom
meant I had nowhere else to go but up.
Thank you for showing me
that I could **climb**.

Control

I know. We want to have control.
We want to take matters into our own hands
and deal with them how we see fit,
but that's not our job.

The sun and rain fall
on the righteous and the evil.
God does not have favorites,
He judges fairly.
The matters
are in His hands.

We are called to *love* one another,
to simply show up
time after time
with an endless and overflowing
heart of acceptance.

It's not about control,
it's about surrender.

Better off

We need to stop getting into relationships
that make us hate ourselves.
We need to stop.

We cannot be in relationships
or have connections with people
who don't see our value
and make us question it.
Out of the billions of people
in this world,
you are with the one person
who doesn't see your value?
How disrespectful to yourself.
How dare you do yourself
a disservice like that?

You know that your confidence
and esteem are essential,
right?
You know that God wants to do amazing
things with your life,
right?
But He can't do any of it
if you can't even see
who you are.
He can't do any of it
if your confidence
is based on other people.

Your priority needs to be
your well-being.
Everyone who's on board,
get on board!
And everyone who's not,
I'm so sorry,
but we've got to leave you in the past.

You better tell yourself
that you are valuable;
you better remind yourself
that God is using you
for something great.

Love is . . .

You gotta know what love is
so that you never get bamboozled or confused
by what it's not.
You gotta know that to love someone
is to value them,
and when you value something,
you cherish it.
You gotta know that to love someone
is to serve them,
to put their needs before your own
and hope that it's returned.

The thing about love
is that it's not earned.
We all deserve love,
so why don't we all receive it?
Because the prerequisite for love is value,
and not everyone is going to see your value,
not everyone is going to see your worth.
But don't ever let their perspective
shift your own.

Earned love

I don't need to earn love,
but you do have to see my value
in order to see the love
that I deserve.

It's not about being a perfect person
to get them to like you.
If they don't see your value,
the love will never follow.
And there is nothing you have to do
to chase it;
the only thing you have to do
is turn the other way
and find someone who values you.

Because love is not earned:
Love is an act of service.
Love is a sacrifice of self.
But you will never understand that
until you value
love.

Boundaries

Self-love means having boundaries.
It's keeping the people who don't know
your worth outside
and the people who cherish your worth inside.
Our boundaries are simply our standards;
they're our standards plastered on our defense,
plastered on our wall:

you can't come in until you meet these criteria
you can't come in until you value who I am
you can't come in until you respect me

It's a caution:

if you don't meet these criteria,
you can't have access to me

Because you having access to me
without meeting these criteria
is what is going to damage me.

Boundaries + vulnerability

I have always been in love with myself.
I just wanted everyone else
to be in love with me too.

When we leave a hole open
for others to fill,
we put our identity in their hands.
This isn't to say that we should
strive to be whole on our own, no.
But this is where the call and need
for boundaries comes in.
If you don't respect me
in the way that I need to be respected,
I can't be around you.
If you don't love me
in the way that I need to be loved,
you can't have access to me.

Not everyone deserves to hold
your loving vulnerability.
Be wise and selective
with who you allow access
to your mind and body.

Real self-love

Self-love isn't only about loving yourself.
Self-love is loving yourself so much
that it spills over into everyone around you.
It's a love that brings service
to your people and the ones who need it the most.
It's seeing the beauty and flaws
that exist within us all
and extending that same grace
you would give yourself
to others.

It's loving on others
the way you would have them
love on you.
Self-love
does not end with the self.

Love is service

We serve
the things we love.

If you love smoking
more than you love stability,
what are you going to do?

If you love your toxic relationship
more than you love
your peace of mind,
what are you going to do?

You're going to serve it, right?

And that's how we end up doing the same things,
just with different people.
That's how we end up fighting the same battles,
just in different fields,
because if you don't love better,
you will never do better.

If you really want change,
if you really want to see a difference in your life,
you must start loving different things.

Start loving different things
and you start doing different things.
Start loving different things
and you start thinking different things.

We serve
the things we love.

Willingness

Love is not love
unless it's a choice.

It cannot be love if it's forced
or manipulated.
Love cannot be love
unless it comes from a place,
a genuine space,
of willing offering.
It's in the willingness of
showing up for someone
who didn't show up for you
or extending an extra hand to someone
who didn't help you.

Love is not love
unless it is a choice.

A real man

A man who respects you
will not try to sleep with you.
A man who wants to protect you
will not try to get
as far as he can with you.

He will ensure an environment
that makes you thrive.
He will build you up
because he understands
that as you grow, so will he.

He understands that a woman
adds to his life,
that she is a prize.
A good thing that is valuable
in many ways.

He will not try and take what he can.
If he values you,
he will respect you.
If he values you,
he will guide you.
If he values you,
he will guard you.

He will ensure the best for you
because he understands
that that is what's best for him.

Strong hearts love harder

I don't think you didn't love me.
I don't think you didn't care,
but I know you took advantage
of me and my kindness.
You abused the love I had for you
and the mountains
that I climbed for you.

Lies.
Deception.
Confusion.
Games.

You played with my mind.
You led me into a pit
when I was blind.
You didn't watch over me.
You didn't guide me.
You led me into the pit that you dug
and made me think
that it was me
who dug it.
You smiled at my misery and
left me alone,
with no map out.

Your wicked ways will not guide me.
Your wicked ways will not lead me
anymore.

An epiphany.
A revelation.
A sudden realization.

Your wicked ways
will only make my heart stronger,
and with a stronger heart,
I will love harder.

You no longer have control.
My heart will do what it does:
It will love.

Love & logic

You blame me for it ending,
but my love is not logical,
my love is not rational;
my love is devoted.
My love is infinite;
my love has no thoughts,
only affection.

My love is not calculated,
my love is unconscious;
my love doesn't fear falling,
my love is brave.

My love is not a cage,
my love is a garden.
Like an island
separated from all norms
but welcoming to all boats.
My love cannot be understood,
only felt.

My love has no pride;
my love is humble.
Its meekness brings dynamics
that the mind cannot fathom
but only the heart can grasp.

Guard your heart

I have a really deep capacity to love.
I know that my level of love,
the depth that I can reach,
is far beyond what I have seen.

And with that
comes responsibility.

A responsibility to guard my heart
and who has access to it.
This isn't an open space.
This isn't a drive-through
that you can just come by
to fill yourself up when you've been feeling low.
I owe it to myself
and everyone around me
to guard my heart.

When my heart is guarded
it's able to be true.
When my heart is guarded
it's able to act in the way
that it was created to.

Yes, your love is deep
and yes, your love is grand,
but it needs to be protected
in order for people
to truly see it stand.

Be like the moon

Be like the moon:
Be there, be constant every night.
Though you shift forms
and show your different sides,
be there, be constant.

Show me your phases and shapes
that change throughout your cycle.
Let me see all that you can be
with all of who you are.

Just like me—
created with a purpose,
spreading light in the darkest of nights—
be my moon,
light up my life.

Where the love is

Go where the love is.
Go where it's warm
and it pours out unconditionally.
Go where the love is patient
and kind,
where it serves to do nothing
but enjoy the space in time.

How often do we chase people
or things
that aren't necessarily
chasing us back?
We strive and fight to be in positions
and places
that don't even allow us
to be ourselves.

There are so many people
who we can't even sit around
with ease.
I don't know what that is
or why that is,
but I do know
that there are people
and places
with so much love to give.

I know that love is freeing and that it allows us
to be ourselves.
And that there is nothing,
nothing quite like the freedom
to be ourselves.

Community love

This life is not about the constant healing and fixing. There is a humanist aspect to us, and there are parts of our humanness that need to be healed not by works but by community and fellowship. I think it's coming into the awareness and understanding that we were put on this planet with other people because we need each other. We need other people to love on us, and other people need us to love on them. So, let's apply the same love we show ourselves to other people. Let's show love to strangers, to our friends and families. They need it too.

Infinite

God is so good.
He gives us
everything we need.
In everything,
we are guided
and protected.

We are guided
even when we take the wrong turn,
we are protected
through the shifts in our mindset,
and our forgiveness
is promised.
No direction too far gone,
no soul too broken
to be embraced
by the ever-flowing
infinite love of God.

Stares at the sunset in awe

Imagine something
as great as the sun
worshiping God
through its service to the world.
Through simply fulfilling
what God has created it to do.

Just like the sun, let's be ourselves.
Let's let our individual lights shine.
Not straining to be brighter
or hurting to do more.
Let's just be
who we were called to be.

Identity

That's the question,
"Who were we called to be?"

A gentle, kind, and patient being
filled with love and
creativity.
God created us to be like Him,
so we only find our identity
through Him.
Through seeking His word
through prayer and
connection.
We find our identity
in what we find
in Him.

Faithful

Don't lose sight of where you are going
because of where you are.
Even when you aren't full and whole,
God's promise remains.

I didn't do what I said I was going to do
and now I'm feeling worthless,
like I don't actually have what it takes.

I said I was going to be consistent,
I said I was going to stick to my word,
and now I'm falling short.

There is no getting around
the challenges of change,
but when we take a step back
and shift our perspective
we start to see the bigger picture.
This moment is not what defines me
but instead
what realigns me.
My standards are getting higher,
my beliefs and my values are evolving.

Know that God is always with you
even when you feel alone
He is with you.

Better days

In my chaos,
God can show me His peace.

In my confusion,
God can show me understanding.

We think that our low moments
are useless.
We think that our low moments
will lead us
astray.
But it's in those moments
that God can show us
His way.

It's in those moments
that we're open
to receive
exactly what it is we need
and to realize
what couldn't be seen
through the eyes
of our looming demise.

It's in those moments
that peace can be felt.
Don't be ashamed
and don't be afraid
of what you are going through
or how you are feeling.

It is an opportunity
for God to light your way
and for you
to see and live
in better days.

His goodness

Everything is going to be okay.
Your heart will heal from the heartbreak,
there will be relief from the grief
of what you thought your life would look like.
Soon you will give birth
to a new reality.
Rest in the fact that with your movement
God is moving too.
He is working it out.

Heart posture

Here's the thing about God:
He isn't focused on our actions
but on the position of our heart
while in action.

When we give,
are we generous only to those
who can pay us back?
If so, are we really generous?
What does that say about our heart?
Did we really give from a place of giving?

When we love,
are we willing to love only the ones
who love us back?
If so, is it really love?
Because loving the ones who love us
is easy;
respecting the ones who respect us
is easy.
Part of life and love is sacrificial.
It's treating people how you
would want to be treated.

God is focused
on the position of our heart
while in action.

Get low

You have to get low
so God can bring you high.
You have to get humble
so God can use you.
So that people
don't have to see through you.

Sometimes we try and strain ourselves into blessings,
not realizing
that on our way, we pick up pride.
On our way, we pick up a complex
of who we are and the status that we hold.
But God never asked you to get high.
He asked you to get low.
He asked you to get low
so that He can reveal Himself
through you.
Get humble.
Get humble enough to accept
what He has for you.

It's not all up to you.
It's not all about the things
that you can do.
Be patient
and allow Him to work through you.

God = love

God is everything good.
Everything good, everything that fills our spirit,
everything that produces love is God.

So when we say God is good,
we aren't saying that He produces good.
We are saying He *is* good.

When we say God is love,
we aren't saying that He produces love.
We are saying He *is* love.

God is the essence of love.
He is the essence of goodness.

The way

I made you this way;
I cannot take it away.
I made you this way;
my grace is your way.
Through your troubles,
my word is the one that guides you.

I made you this way,
and so you don't have to fight
or hide it.
There is purpose in what you see
as burden;
there is hope in what you see
as defeat.

I made you this way,
so there is no other way
to find your way.

Heavy hearts and minds

To all the heavy hearts and minds
that never seem to find
a place to resign:
I hope you know
that what you think and feel
is real.
I hope you know that time will pass,
and as it does,
you can relax.
I hope you know that this is not
all that there is,
that you will find
your peace of mind,
that you can be
more than what you think and feel.

I hope you know that redemption is real.
That anything
(and I mean anything)
can be made right
if you step into
the light.
Don't be afraid,
don't be discouraged.
There is so much for you
on the side of faith and hope.
On the side of light and life.

Feel what you have to feel,
but remember,
anything can be made right.

In process

It's all a part of the process.
The struggle is a part of the growth,
the pain is a part of the healing,
the trust is a part of the rebuilding.

When you feel like the struggle
is getting too big
or the pain too strong
and you have nothing left to give,
remind yourself
that the very moment
you feel like giving up or doubting yourself
is the moment
that true transformation
begins.

It was never going to be easy,
and it was never going to be comfortable,
but rest in the fact that
when you feel opposition,
you are surely in the process
of growing.

Remember that your strength
doesn't have to come from you.
It can come from God
and His goodness.

Give it to God

I know it's easier said than done,
but trust and believe that your life
has purpose.
Trust and believe that God
has not forgotten about you.
If there's something you want to do,
if there is something heavy on your heart
or on your mind,
pray.

Pray and give it to God.
Do not be anxious about anything,
because He is there waiting for you
to call on Him.
He is there waiting
for you to lean on Him.

The truth is that you have purpose,
and you are going to do so many things in this life,
but in order for you to do them,
God needs you to be in your full essence.
Give Him your stress,
give Him your worry, and
give Him your anxiety
so that He can use you.
You are useful,
for the goodness of the world
and for the love that radiates
through your life.

More

It's just where you are, not who you are.
You might be in a place of misalignment
and so far away from God,
but that does not define who you are:
It is simply where you are.

The fact that you were created
and living in this world
is a clear indication
that you are here
for a reason.
That your existence
has purpose.
And that purpose is revealed
through your relationship with God;
that purpose is revealed
through finding out who you really are.

You are more than your pain.
You are more than your confusion.
You are more than your lack of confidence.
There is a reason that you are here,
and you've got to find that out.
Because it will turn your life around.
It will brighten your days
and pave your way forward.

The journey

Something like my
intuition.

God speaks to me through my
transition.

I know that I can trust Him; faith is my
religion.

UNCERTAINTY

Uncertainty

I'm no longer fighting the uncertainty.
I'm not giving up on any of my dreams
or my ambitions, but
I'm loosening my grip.

I'm leaving room for greater,
or lesser in some areas,
because I'm realizing
that life in my control
is kind of shitty.

It's filled with anxiety.
It's filled with overthinking
and trying to control
everything.

And if I'm being honest,
I just want to rest in the ebbs and flows.
I want to be a real person.
I want to enjoy when it's good
and hate when it's bad
because that's what life is:
contrast.

It's taking my foot off the gas
and coasting through the mundane.
It's shifting gears and taking it
day by day.

I'm no longer fighting the uncertainty.
I am choosing to have faith
through it all.

In flow

Big highs come with big lows,
but I'd rather stay in flow.
I'd rather watch things grow
without me taking control.
I'd rather take a seat,
not to sit back and relax
but to do all that I have to do
without the grand expectation
of an outcome that is out of my control.

I'd rather let each piece play its role
beyond my understanding.
Let it come together
without all my planning.
Because it's limited
and it's skewed,
it doesn't always have
the best point of view.

I'd rather let it go,
let it go and find my flow
rather than living
in the peaks and valleys.
I'd rather find peace
in what I don't understand,
release the grip of my hand
on the plan that will eventually
and inevitably
come to unfold
in a way that is greater
and more grand
than any story
I could have ever told.

Spiritual

It's spiritual,
you're not meant to know
and understand everything.
When you're trying to figure out
why certain things didn't play out,
also understand that some things
are working for your good,
but they are working
beyond your understanding.
They are working
beyond what you can think
and feel.

They're coming together
in perfect harmony
for you to one day look back
and say,

"Oh, I understand, I understand
why it had to play out that way.
I'm grateful for everything I learned through it.
I'm grateful for everything that missed me, because
everything that missed me also showed me me."

One day you're going to be in a place
where everything makes sense
and all your questions
have been answered.
But in the meantime,
you must make peace
with the unknown.

Come together

Have faith.
Even when you don't see it,
believe it.
Be strong
in what you feel within you.
Don't let anyone's opinion
shift your direction.
Know that this is spiritual
beyond what can be
explained.
You are stronger than you think.
You are capable.
Keep believing, keep pushing,
and keep having faith.
It will make sense one day.
It will all come together.

Comfort in purpose

I realized that purpose
is my comfort.
I could have everything I want,
but if I don't have a purpose,
I don't even want it.
I could have all the fancy things
and take all the cool trips
but still find myself in cities
wishing I had something
to stand for.
Wishing that there was something
deeper and bigger
behind it all.

I realized that I'm happiest
when I'm on purpose.
When I'm working hard
and in the direction of a vision,
that is when the balance flows in,
when I can work and play
and play without thinking about work.
Because I know that I am on purpose,
I know that this moment
of relaxation and rest
pours into the plan.

I can enjoy.
I can laugh.
I can find beauty,
because I know that it will last.

Find yourself again

How is God going to use you
if you're not even you?
How is God going to use you
if you're in a relationship
that makes you hate everything about yourself?

Sometimes we get into relationships
and form attachments that blind us,
blind us from the reality of who we are.
We used to be happy-go-lucky.
All of a sudden, we're pessimistic.
We used to have passions and ambitions.
All of a sudden, we can't see a way.

The relationships we have are instrumental;
the people we speak and spend time with
are instrumental.
God wants to use you
and your essence.
He wants to use all those things
that you call flaws;
He calls them opportunities.
Opportunities for Him to draw you in closer.
Opportunities for Him
to restore your sense of self and confidence.
Remember that He needs you to be you
in order to use you.
So be brave,
be brave enough to ***find yourself again.***

Nice to myself

I'm starting to be nice to myself again.
I'm starting to understand
that my past is my past
and my future
is endless.
Endlessly abundant with possibilities
both good and bad
but fruitfully filled
with every aching bone,
every tear that I shed alone.

I'm starting to be kind to myself again.
Allowing myself to play in the unknown,
not punishing myself for the things
that I don't condone.
I know that I am not alone.
I am guided.
I am protected.
Even when I stray,
I know that I'm not really prey.

There is so much ahead of me.
I refuse to let my past,
I refuse to let my mistakes,
take this growing place,
take this fruitful case,
and keep it in one place.

I'm starting to be nice to myself again
and I'm grateful,
I'm so grateful
that I learned through the things
that I yearned.

Louder faith

I don't have to know it all,
and I don't have to have
all the answers.
I don't have to make sense of it
or understand it fully.
I can just show up.

I can be present in this moment,
taking in what's in front of me
and letting go of what is not.

I don't have to figure it all out.
I don't have to take
everything as a sign
and make it all align.
I can just live freely in this moment.

Knowing that everything will come
together
beyond my understanding,
beyond my orchestration.
I'm tired of being tired,
of living in frustration.
Life is more than just getting it right.
It's having faith
even when you don't.

Scared to get lost

I'm not scared of relationships,
I'm scared of myself.
I'm scared of losing sight of my values
and morals
for the sake of love
or the idea of love.
Love is something that sets you free,
free from the expectations
of what love
is supposed to be.
So, I'm not scared of relationships.
I'm scared of straying off the path
into a relationship
that brings me further away from myself.
That covers and distracts my purpose,
my essence, my natural vibrancy for life.
I'm scared of losing sight,
getting lost in the direction
of what seems to be right.

Matthew 5:4

God blesses those who mourn, for they will be comforted.

Through the lived experience of pain,
of grief,
of sorrow,
comes comfort and understanding.
Healing comes from moving through the pain.

In order to heal we must feel.
We can grow and evolve
into the best versions of ourselves.
We can move past our pain and suffering,
but in order to do that,
we have to feel it first.

Rest in the fact that
your comfort is promised through your mourning:
through the *mourning of your loved ones,*
through the *mourning of your old self,*
through the *mourning of your old habits.*

Your comfort lies on the other side
of moving through your pain.

As you go

Don't let your confidence hold you back from who you are. People are going to have opinions, but your confidence and self-assurance need to be louder. Start to build that confidence by building your faith and believing, even sometimes without seeing. Walk into those rooms with your head held high. Even when you don't feel it, know that you belong. Share your opinion and say what you have to say. Even when you aren't fully confident, do it anyway.

The best way to learn is by doing, and sometimes our confidence just isn't there, but that does not mean that there is nothing to do. That we can't try and learn from our mistakes. Don't be afraid to take the chance and be confident. Know that you can learn as you go.

The mundane

Fighting the mundane
is kind of like fighting the day-to-day.
The more you fight it, the more it attacks.
The more you embrace it,
the more you learn to relax.

The mundane is a part of our lives.
It's the part that is boring
and lackluster,
but it's also the part
where we learn the most.

Where our mind has extra time
and our body has strength.
Where do we find our peace
when it's no longer a threat?
When it's calm and it's quiet.
When it's clear and it's still.
Is the reflection we see what we hope to mirror?

The magic of the mundane
is in the reflection that we find.

Don't let it get to you

Half of the battle is in not letting it get to you.
What is for you is for you;
keep going.
Keep moving forward
until you find out,
because you will.

You will understand why you are the way you are.
You will understand why it happened
the way it happened,
why you had to feel what you had to feel.
Remember that half the battle
is in how it gets to you.

Don't let it crush you; don't let it kill your spirit.
There is so much more for you to give.
There is so much more for you to offer
to yourself, to all the amazing people around you
who want and love to see you thrive.

You are purposeful.
Don't let the struggle
blind the reality of who you are
and where you're going.
Don't let it get to you.

Faith

If you are going to outside sources
to validate yourself or the direction you're headed,
you don't have faith.
You are soaking up all the opinions
of the people around you,
allowing them to confirm or deny
who you are.
That is not faith.
And it's time you start to say it,
because in order to find
what you don't already have,
you have to first admit
that you're missing it.
Recognize your lack of faith
in order to start developing it.

Spiritual rest

I rest in the fact that God's plans
are bigger than my own.
If I can think and dream up
all these amazing possibilities
for my life and how they'll play out,
just imagine what God's dreaming.
Just imagine
the plans that He has
that are greater than my understanding,
that exceed my expectations.
I simply rest in the fact
that I can dream.
I can get excited about my future,
but the final destination
is greater than my imagination.

I surrender to His plans for my life.

Love God

Let me love God
more than I love intimacy.
Let me love God
more than I love being
in a relationship.

A lot of the time we get off track
because we actually love the things
that destroy us
more than we love
what's for us.

We can't even see
that what's for us
is better than what destroys us,
so what do we do?
We blindly walk into misalignment.
We blindly walk into the arms
of what seems like love
but what actually
pulls us further away
from real happiness.

So I'm building a relationship with God
that is so intimate and so authentic
that I can say,
I know God,
and I know that what He has for me
is greater than anything I can desire.

And when the temptation rises
and I feel like backsliding,
I remind myself of who I love.
I love the one who loves me most.

Matured faith

The journey was never meant to be easy.
You were never meant
to have it all figured out,
to have and keep all the answers.
Sometimes we learn things,
and then we forget.

Sometimes our beliefs
and our faith spark up,
and then they spark down
just as fast.

We thought we understood,
we thought we found solid ground,
but we've been humbled
to the fact that real faith
takes time.
Real faith is a work in progress.
It takes time for its roots
to form and mature,
so don't be discouraged.
When you feel like you've
lost your footing,
don't give up.
You know what you saw and felt.
You know that it was real.
Don't let your past
or your mess-ups
hold you back.
Do not give in to the temptation
of the easy life.

We need you.
We need you to persevere.
We need your matured faith.

For the good

At the end of the day,
everything is always working
for the good.

I can be in my darkest moments,
in the worst phase of my life
with no way out,
but I know that everything
is working for the good.
I know that, even in my darkness,
God is completing the puzzle.
He's looking at the pieces
and fitting them together.
He's using the darkness
that I'm in and saying,
How can I turn this around?
How can I fit this piece into my great plan?

I remind myself
that, even though I can't see it,
even though I might not be able
to feel it in this moment,
He is working.
Whether I wallow or smile in my pain,
He is working for the good.

Faith over frequency

You cannot manifest God's plan.
God's plan calls for patience.
His plan calls for total trust
in His love and protection
and faith in His goodness.

If you believe in God
and all of His mighty love for you,
and this world, and your life,
then you must also believe
that in your surrender,
in giving God the total authority
over your life,
comes His plan and His promise.

Sometimes we think we know
better than God.
I know what I need, I know what and
who will be good for me.
I know which direction to take
and which way to go.

We get so caught up
in our pride and our ego,
we think we know what's best,
so we try to *manifest.*
But if you believe in God,
there is no manifesting.
There is only surrender.

Fully

If God is the only one
who knows me fully,
why would I not trust
that His plan
is the only plan
that would fill my life?
Why would I not trust
that His plan
is the only plan
that would sustain me?
That His wisdom
and His guidance
over my life
is the greatest
protection?
Why would I not have faith
that His plan
has my best interest at heart?

Jaded

I don't want anything that I want.
Everything that I've ever wanted
never wanted me,
never wanted to serve
my highest self.

A lot of times, I hear people say:
I get whatever I want.
I can manifest it, I can alchemize it,
I can bring it into fruition.

And yes, these things are true,
but do you really need
what you want?
Is what you want
really what you need?

What I'm realizing now
is that I want everything
that God wants for me.
God has the bird's-eye view
over my life,
so I don't want what I want.
My vision is clouded.
My vision is jaded.
I want everything that God wants for me.

Proverbs 2:3-5

Cry out for insight, and ask for understanding. Search for them as you would for silver; seek them like hidden treasures. Then you will understand what it means to fear the Lord, and you will gain knowledge of God.

How did you find God?

She answered:

"God finds us in our broken places. It's in those moments of genuinely seeking refuge and answers that we find the understanding we need. It takes a humble spirit to gain wisdom. Matter of fact, it takes a humble spirit to learn anything at all. You don't have to be going through a crisis to grow, but you do need to have faith in what you are looking for. If you want to find God, stop questioning and start listening. Humble yourself to the point of receiving what can't otherwise be received through a knowing heart."

Peace

Finding peace within the storm
is like finding faith within the darkness.

I don't know how my life will play out,
but I have faith that it will be good.

I don't know when this feeling will pass,
but I have faith that it will.

That alone brings me peace.
We don't know exactly how life will play out.
We don't know how it will turn out in the end,
but having faith and believing
that it will work out for the good
is what brings us peace.
The thing about peace is that it's infinite.
In a state of peace, when our mind is at ease,
it can drift and think and dream.
When we are at peace,
and our mind is in a state of calm,
from there
we can see everything clearly.
From there,
we can do anything.

Less reactions

Less reactions
to the opinions of others.
Less reactions
to the skewed perspectives
they hold.
Sometimes we can feel out of balance,
like everything about us
is changing.
Your *perspective* is changing,
your *interests* are changing,
your *values* are changing—
everything is shifting.

And with that comes a clash
of the old and the new.
But remember,
every time you have grown
and changed,
you have also
gotten closer
to yourself.

Vices

The things we do in hiding
love to stay in hiding.
What is done in the dark
stays covered by the darkness.

Similarly, our vices don't like good things.
They don't like the uncovering
that comes with the light.
A lack of self-control doesn't like rules or restrictions;
a lack of patience doesn't like waiting;
a lack of discipline doesn't like order or structure;
a lack of peace doesn't like understanding.

Our vices don't like good things.
So there is going to be a tug,
there is going to be a pull
between our old selves and our new selves.
Our old ways and our new ways.
Remember that growth
is on the other side
of what doesn't feel good.
It's on the other side
of comfort.

Lessons learned

I know that the degree of my challenges
are equal to the degree of my growth.
I know that the wave
of overwhelming sadness
and the grief I'm going through
are only going to produce
that exact same wave
of growth.

I know that this season of bottomless despair,
this season of pain,
is followed by my season of growth.
If this pain is as heavy as it is,
I know that when I get through it,
when I understand what's really going on,
I know that I'm going to grow
just as much as I suffered.
Because nothing is in vain,
and everything can be used
for good.

Anxiety

The anxiety you are going through
is not your identity.

You are not your anxiety.

You have patterns and tendencies to
overthink and worry,
and you've been doing it for years.
Some of us have even been taught to
see life through fear,
but know that this is not your identity.
What is planned for you is greatness;
what is within you is greatness.
And you will walk into that greatness
regardless of the fears you have.
Have faith;
move in love and hope.

Depression

The depression that you are going through
is not your identity.

You are not your sadness.

You are filled with so much beauty and light,
and trust me when I say it
because everyone around you can see it.
You have so many people who love you.
You have so many people who see your worth;
they are just waiting for you to see it too.

So wake up and walk with your head held high.
Know that this is not your identity
but simply something you're working through.
Have faith.
Brighter days are coming.

Small victories

It's in the small victories
that we find the strength
to carry on.
That we're filled with newfound wisdom
to push through to the next chapter of our journey.

If you are fighting to break a habit,
working toward changing your life
by way of mind
or spirit,
whatever it may be,
remember that it's in the small victories.
It's in simply saying no
and forcing yourself to turn away
when all you want to do
is turn toward comfort.
It's in fighting those two minutes,
those two minutes of wanting to give in,
that you're filled
with the wisdom
and the knowledge
to carry you through.

A lot of times, we think it's in our motives,
our intentions to do good,
but let me tell you,
it's in our actions.
So be strong,
find new strengths in old weaknesses,
and know that even when you give in,
you can try again.
There is still hope.
There is still time.

Self-control

Don't always follow your heart.
Remember to have
self-control.

There are seasons
ordained for different reasons,
reasons that oftentimes
aren't fully understood within the season.
The *why* isn't always
understood,
but the *how*
calls for self-control.

How do I respond to opportunities
within a season of drought?
How do I cater to those around me
when God has so graciously
catered to me?

How we respond to life
is a reflection of our self-control.

Enough

All you can do is your best,
and I know you may not believe this,
but your best is enough.

Your best is enough to get you through the day.
Your best is enough to get you through the door
and, contrary to popular belief,
your best is all you have to do.

The greatest motivation
comes from seeing your own progress,
so continue to move forward
until you start to realize
just how strong you are.
Because you are strong,
and you are capable of getting through
whatever it is you're going through.

It isn't going to be easy,
and it won't always make sense,
but trust that everything will work out.
Trust that everything is coming together
in time
and that everything—
everything—
will eventually
be just fine.

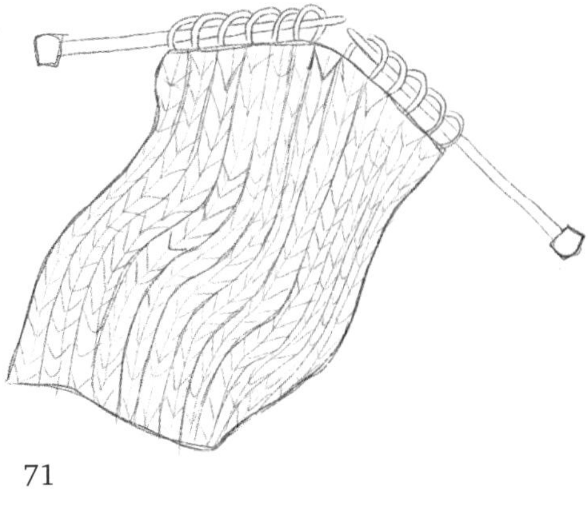

Useful

God does not make anything useless.
While you're looking at your life
and comparing it to everyone else's,
know that the struggles and pains on your path,
the ups and downs that you think are so in vain,
are put in place for a reason.

Your path is rigid for a reason;
start to look around and see what you can learn.
Start to look around at all the broken pieces,
everything that didn't hold.
See how you can use them
for something good.

The struggles we face
are building us up to be
who we were meant to be.
Stop fighting the struggle
and accept it,
turn it around, and learn from it.
Apply it and have faith that
the future will be bright.
Have faith that this isn't the end.

Maintaining hope

Always have hope
and know that you are never alone.
Try your best
and know that God will take care of the rest.
Be honest and transparent with your heart.
Pray for clarity and revision.
Because sometimes life gets overwhelming
when we're stuck in the same cycles of
our past.
But know that life is an open-ended journey
and nothing is destined to be
except what sets you free.
Root yourself in faith
and guard yourself in hope.
Keep moving forward
toward your future,
which is bright.

INSIGHT

Can't change people

The goal is not to change people
but to see if we can accept
who they already are.

People will show you
who they are,
and a common mistake
we make
is trying to change
what we see.

The question you should ask is,
"Can I accept who they are?"
"Is this someone or something I can work with?"
There is no bargaining
with who they are.
There is no changing
a personality
that is already formed.
You must shift your mindset to,
"Can I accept the person standing in front of me?"
"Do I respect this person?"
The answer to these questions
will guide your actions.
They will determine
your willingness to accept.

Impossible

It's impossible
for one person
to have every lived experience.
It's impossible
for you to fully know and understand
what other people are going through.
It's impossible
for you to really live in their shoes.

The next time you want to judge
and look down on others
to boost your own ego,
remember that what you see
is half of what truly is.
What you see
is what they choose to show you.

Be kind and have a little more patience.
Be wise and look beneath the surface
because within us all
is a story that hasn't been told.
Within us all
is a story that's dying
to be accepted.

Listen

More listening, less opinions.
So often, we try to understand
by rationalizing,
by putting our own understanding
on things that are beyond us,
that exceed our ability to comprehend.

More listening, less opinions.

This is a practice I'm taking with me.
This is what I'm marking on my heart.

Not everything you think
needs to be said.
Not everything you feel
needs to be shared.
Some things are beyond you,
beyond your understanding,
beyond your comprehension.
Your opinion, your beautiful thoughts and perspective,
as true as they may seem to you,
lack understanding
and the ability
to portray what is true.

So be kind;
be slow to speak
and quick to listen.
You will learn so much more
from accepting
rather than projecting
and rejecting.

Stop believing the lies

You have to stop believing the lies.
You have to stop believing the thoughts
that come into your mind and suddenly
become a part of who you are.

You were not put on this planet to be small.
You were not put on this planet
to live in the shadows of your potential.
You were created with a God-given potential
and a greatness already within you.

Anything that comes against that
and triggers you into being small,
it's got to move to the side,
it's got to move to the back
so that your fullness can move forward.
So that your light can be shown.

It was never about searching
and finding your identity
but instead
uncovering who you were created to be.
Uncovering the light that was always within you.
Stop believing those lies
and stop believing those triggers
that hold a part of your identity.

Doubts

Okay, I know those thoughts are coming in again.
I know you're starting to doubt yourself.
You're starting to doubt your abilities
and the direction
that you're headed in.

You look back
and all you can see
is the success you somehow managed
to achieve.
You're feeling as if it's over.
You're feeling as if it might be time
to just lie low.

But listen:
The mind is a fickle place,
and even when those feelings come up
and you feel like letting them take control,
remember that you can move through them.
Remember that you can still show up
with doubts in your mind.

I know you feel out of place,
like everything you're doing
is a waste,
but you can move through it.
You've got to push forward
with the same energy
and capacity as you did before,
and eventually
your mind will catch up,
and you will find ease
once more.

Consideration

Imagine what it would be like
if we took the opinions of others
and used them only as consideration.
Considering what they have to say,
receiving what they have to say,
but still knowing
that it is not the final say.

A new day

Remind yourself that today
is a new day.
A new opportunity
to fill yourself with all the joys
that come with life.
Today is not the day
to let your pain
hold you back.
It's not the day
for your memories
to keep you in the past.
It is an opportunity,
to look toward the horizon
of endless opportunities
and soak up all the blessings
that you have been given.

Despite all that you have been through,
you have made it this far.
I promise you
the journey does not end today.
It is an opportunity
to find your presence and stay in it.
Today is a new and wondrous day.

Get out of your mind

The second we compare ourselves to others,
we get out of our body
and into our mind.
And our mind
is a universe.

It's vast, it's large,
it's an endless space
that can take us in any direction
and oftentimes
leaves us in darkness.

The second you find yourself overthinking
or comparing yourself to someone else's
success,
lifestyle,
relationship,
remember to get out of your mind and
back into your body.
You might have to get up
and start physically moving.
You might have to switch up your environment:
Get off your phone,
get off the couch,
and get into the real world,
start socializing.
Because you cannot stay in your mind.
Your mind without movement
is stagnant.
It's constantly feeding
on your fears.

Purposeful

Comparison can be a slippery slope.
It makes everyone but yourself
competition
and puts you in a race
with the entire world
when you already have a race
to win from within.
You already have your own challenges
and obstacles to overcome.
Comparison does nothing
but distract you
from what's on your path.

Remember that what's in front of you
is the key to your success.
What is in front of you
is the roadmap
to your own unique purpose.

Don't allow comparison
to distract you.
Don't allow what other people are doing
to distract you from what you've got to do.

Purpose is not a destination;
it's not a place that you can get to.
Your purpose is your life.
It's waking up and choosing to be
the best version of yourself,
taking all the micro actions
and thoughts
and filtering them in order to be
the light that you're called to be.

It's accepting the past
and moving toward the future,
taking all that you have been through,
and turning those lessons
into future blessings.

Your purpose is not a destination;
it's all the steps
along the way.
The lessons you learn
and the interactions you have,
they're meaningful
beyond your understanding.
They bring purpose,
from day to day.

Comparison

No one wins from comparison because even when you put yourself above others, you still separate yourself. As human beings, it's in our nature to want to feel connected and loved, and when you put yourself above others, you separate yourself. When you put yourself below others, you also separate yourself. So stop comparing, because it does nothing but isolate you. It does nothing but separate you when what you really want is to feel connected.

Superpower

Your essence
is your **superpower.**
Nobody has been through
what you have been through,
seen what you have seen,
or felt what you have felt.
It might have been similar,
it might have been close,
but it wasn't the same.

Your uniqueness is what sets you apart.
It's a compilation of all the quirks
that make up *you.*
Your introspection
and way of processing the world
creates your unique story.

Unless someone has lived
the **exact** same life as you,
your essence will **always** be
your superpower.
Because nobody else
got it the same way you did.

To be understood

A lot of times, we subconsciously carry a list of the expectations that we have of others. When those expectations clash with reality, we start to relate differently. We start to see people for who they really are. Not what we expected or what we wanted, not the parts we imagined would fill us—we start to see the real person. And if you want to be seen truly and fully, you have to tell people where you are. You have to act in a manner that is in alignment with your beliefs so that, when they see you and their perspective no longer shifts, you know that you've found someone that is truly looking at you.

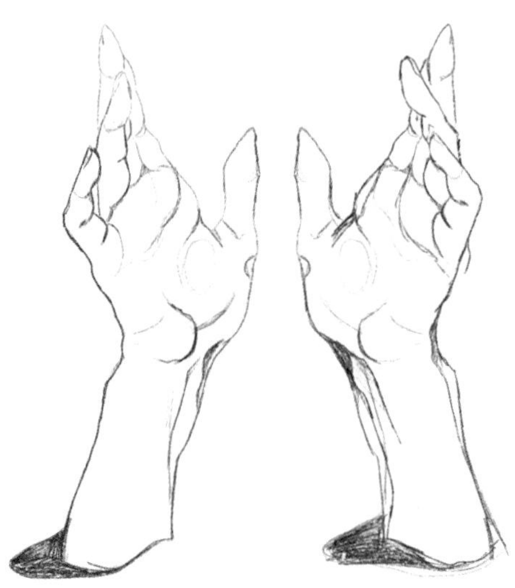

See me

If me telling you where I'm at
changes the way that you see me,
then you were never really looking at me.
You were looking at the idea
that you had of me,
the way I may have presented myself,
but you were never really looking at me.

This is for all the people
who try to hide who they are,
who try to live under the mask
of what they think is protection.
This is for the people
who are grieving a connection
or the rejection that came from being true to
yourself.
If that is what pushes people away,
then that connection
was never really true.
It never really belonged to you.

Yes, the emotions were real, and the attachment
might have been there,
but it was never really true.
They were never really looking
at you.

Do the hard things

Do the hard things.
You can never go wrong by doing the right thing.
This is what guides me when my discipline
is running low.
Do the hard things.
Say how you feel when you know that it's real.
Be honest even when it's easier to lie and get by.
Be straight up with your feelings
even when it makes you feel small.
Because doing the right thing
even when it doesn't feel like it
will always take you further.
It will clear your path
and your conscience.

Your kindness isn't silly

We're afraid to be kind and nice to others because we're afraid that it'll be taken as weakness. Think about a time when someone did something nice for you. You didn't deserve it, and it wasn't called for, but as you received their kindness, you started to soften. You wondered, *Why are there such kind people in this world? Why did they just do this for no reason? Hmm, maybe I should be one of them too.* The feeling of receiving what you didn't deserve or earn is like no other. It's visceral, mental, and literally fills your spirit. If you are ever in a situation debating what to do, remember what it felt like to be given kindness when you didn't deserve it. Let that guide your actions, and hopefully you won't feel so silly being kind.

Actions

I can't ask you if you'll respect me,
but I can see it.
I can't ask you if you'll protect me,
but I can see it.
Stop relying on what people say
and start to look at what they do.

Our actions are more true
to how we feel and what we carry in our heart.
Actions tell it all.

Don't feel defeated
and don't settle for a lack of autonomy.
You can use your judgment
and see
where people truly are
and how they choose
to play their part.

Look-alike

Everyone knows what love is "supposed" to look like.
Everyone knows what a relationship
is "supposed" to feel like.

So anyone can show you exactly what you crave,
and anyone can tell you
exactly what you long to hear.
The key is not soaking up everything you hear
but instead allowing people the opportunity
to show up in the way that you need them to.
Allowing people to show up in accordance
with the words that they say
and the promises
that they make.

It's not about the words: It's about how their words
line up with their actions.

Who you are

Not everybody is going to see your worth,
not everybody is going to treat you
the way that you deserve,
but regardless of how people see you,
what matters most
is how you see yourself.

Do you know that you are valuable?
Do you know that your worth exists
beyond the compliments?

Because it's knowing this
that protects and maintains your identity.
People will come into your life
with all kinds of perspectives,
and they will treat you
how they see fit.
But it is not your job
to fit someone else's narrative.
It is not your job to conform
to how people see or treat you.

You are independent of anyone else's
opinion, comment, or perspective.
Your value comes from a place of truth.
Your value comes from an authentic place within.

Don't ever let how someone treats you
define you.
Remember who you are;
remember that you are valuable
regardless of who sees it.

Your body is sacred

When you give someone access to your body,
you give them access to your mind.
You give them access to the way you see yourself
and the way you see the world.

Giving someone access to your mind is saying:

*You can come into this place that holds my vision.
This place that holds my dreams, my hope for the
future, my confidence, my self-worth, and my identity.
You can come into this sacred place, this place that
holds everything that I am and everything that I was
created to be.*

But you also need to remember
that not everyone is equipped to navigate
through life with you.
Not everyone is going in the same direction as you.
Not everyone is going to see all the purpose
within your sacred place.

Your mind and body are connected.
Make sure that they are protected.

Scraps

Don't settle for the scraps
of what people are willing to give you
for the attention
that will momentarily fill you.

Attention feels good.
Attention feels so good
that we are willing to give up our peace of mind
to occupy our time with momentary connection.
But you have to remember
that what you are really looking for
is not in the attention you receive.

What you are really looking for
is in the connection that develops over time.
It's in the intimacy of being seen.
What actually needs to fill your void
is commitment.
What actually needs to fill your void
is acceptance.
I know the attention feels safe,
I know the attention feels like it's
filling you with what you need,
but the attention isn't going to bring you peace.
The attention isn't going to fill that missing piece
that you so desperately need
to be free.

Respect yourself

It is not an act of service
to sell yourself short.
It is not an act of service
to give yourself away
to people
who don't see your worth.

You think that it's naive,
that it's cute,
that people should owe you
because you respect them.
But there is nothing honorable
in being small,
in failing to recognize the worth
that God has put in you.

Where is the respect when it
comes to you and what you
deserve?
Where is the honor when it
comes to living up to who you
are?

There is nothing to be praised
about your insecurity,
your lack of self-worth,
and your inability
to see and demand it
in everything you do.

The way you start to look at
yourself
is the way you teach others
to see you too.

True value

You can say all the wonderful things
and paint a beautiful picture
with your words,
but if your actions don't align,
is it really true?
Many times
we fall into the deception
of the words we hear,
not knowing that actions
are what make them true.

Understand that it takes effort
to put an idea into action.
Just like starting something new,
we can't just talk about it:
We have to actually be about it.

It takes dedication to show up
and follow through.
It's in the actions
that we find the truth.
It's how we show up
that defines who we are.

Don't be deceived
by the words that you hear
or even the words
that you tell yourself.
Know that the truth
lies within your actions.
Your actions
have true value.

Independent

Your worth is not dependent
on what anyone says about you.
Your value
does not come from the approval
of other people
or the validation
that you find.
On the days when you feel small,
your value remains.
On the days when you feel like giving up,
you have it within you
to keep going and pushing forward.
You are not a subject of your feelings.
You are more than your day-to-day struggles,
in the midst of them
you can prosper.
In the midst of them
you can thrive.

Strength in real form

You showed me my shortcomings,
thinking it would keep me down,
but now it's the thing
that keeps me off the ground.

Impactful lessons
come from seeing the sides we tried to hide.
I thought that my kindness was strength,
until I realized
that it could be used against me.
The strength that filled my identity
and sense of self
wasn't the best.
It was a guise,
a guise I used in hopes
that other people
wouldn't feel the need
to use me.
Or call on their morality:
"How dare you mistreat me?
How dare you do this to me
when all I've been was nice to you?"
My kindness was a shield,
a shield that guarded my weakness
and inability to see or deal
with what was real.

You must have the strength within
to be harsh and speak up for yourself,
to say no and walk away.
That is kindness without weakness.
That is strength in real form.

Speckled

The way people treat you
is not a reflection of your worth.
Most times
it's a reflection
of what's within them.

We are each living in our own world,
coming together in this world,
trying to figure it out together.
We each see life
through our uniquely speckled lenses.
Our lenses have been marked
by the winds
of our life.
They've been marked
by the paths we've crossed
and the experiences we've had.

They affect how we connect.
Most of our interactions
are simply reflections of our markings.
It's not always personal.

Confidence

We have got to stop caring
what other people think about us.
Sometimes we seek so much outside validation
because we're waiting for them
to give us the permission
to be ourselves.
This is a life lived
at the mercy of outside approval.

When we base our confidence on the validation
and approval of others,
we give them the key to our happiness.
We place our identity and our self-worth
at the mercy of their approval.
If they dislike me, I'm worthless.
If they like me, I'm valuable.
We give others the power to define our identity
when we base our confidence on their approval.

Remember that you are a whole human being
with thoughts and ideas.
That your confidence should be based
on how you feel about yourself,
how you think about yourself.
You define who you are
not anyone else.

Different

I found the space to be me.
I'm no longer looking at others
and questioning who I am
in comparison to who they are.

I found the space to be different.

I admire your style and beauty.
As different as it is from mine,
it doesn't take from
or add to who I am.

I found the safety to feel secure.

In my style or lack thereof,
in my expression
or how I wear my hair.
Whatever I choose to wear, I know I'm still me.
Underneath all these layers,
it's me.

It's me, and I don't have to prove myself.

I remember
that, in all your glory,
there is still space
for me to be me.

I embrace who I am.
I embrace all the differences
that make me *me*.

I am enough. I am just right.

Resonate

The people who resonate with you
are the ones who are thinking
about you.
To resonate with someone
is to feel them, to understand them deeply.

It isn't the people who think you're weird
or corny and don't get your vibe
who are thinking about you.
Trust me, they're not wasting more than a second
ruminating on your so-called "weirdness."

There is absolutely no reason
for you to hide who you are
for fear of judgment.
The people who don't get you
are simply passing by,
but the ones who resonate
are the ones who matter.
They are the ones we should be focusing on.

Embrace it

Just be yourself.
Don't miss out on the fullness of life
because you're afraid to be who you really are.
Embrace the things you feel shy
and awkward about.
There's nothing worse than hiding who you are
because you think other people won't accept you.
You have no idea who will accept you.
You have no idea who will love the things
that you somehow hate about yourself.

Allow other people the opportunity
to gravitate toward you.
Allow yourself the opportunity
to live in the fullness of you.

Perfectly imperfect

I am not anxiety, depression, or ADHD.
I am __________ (fill in your name),
and __________ is sensitive.

I see and smell something new,
and all of a sudden, I feel blue.

I get overwhelmed
and stimulated quickly,
but it is a part of my wit.

Yes, I struggle to find my way,
but in due time, I'll be okay . . .

I am not a list of issues,
and it's in realizing this
that I can actually move.

Through the days that feel like night
and the nights that feel like fights.
I can find my grounding
in knowing
that I am more than my surroundings.

I am not a list of things.
I am simply perfectly imperfect.

You are capable

Did you know that you are capable
of anything you put your mind to?

Did you know
that your thoughts and fears
are just symptoms
of what you've heard?
Anytime you have an idea, an ambition,
something you want to bring into fruition,
I need you to remember
that your fears, your doubts, your second guesses
are not facts.

We need you,
we need you and all of your ideas.
We need you and all of your essence.
We need you in this world,
so don't get stuck in your mind,
and don't get stuck in the chaos
of whatever it's telling you.

Realest

Beauty comes from within.
It comes from a humble and kind
and gentle spirit.

Beauty comes
from being a good friend.

Beauty comes
from being a good neighbor.

Your beauty
is not what's on the outside;
that fades and runs out.
Your beauty
comes from within;
it shines eternally.
It shines forever.

Focus on what's within
and watch how it shines
through all your insecurities.

The truth

The truth settles my soul.
It fills me with so much conviction
that all the outside noise
starts to fade away.

The thing about truth
is that it has its way
of settling us into the bigger picture.
And that's all we need to get a better look
at our situation and all the moving pieces
to understand where and how we went wrong.

The truth is not something to be afraid of.
The truth is comforting.
It has the ability to show us reality
from a different perspective.

In its essence,
the truth is healing.

Cherished

We idolize the things we cherish most.
In relationships, we idolize our partners.
In success, we idolize the money
or the status that comes with it.

What we cherish becomes our idol;
it becomes our driving force.
And the thing about idolizing *things* or *people*
is that they're always out of our control.
Much of life is about accepting the things
we can't control,
and it's scary to lose control,
but that's where faith comes in.

Where we rely on a higher source,
a higher power—
God—
to carry us through the uncertainty.
We don't have to idolize what we cherish;
we can idolize the one in control of what we cherish.
And through that
we can find a little bit of peace.

Avoid pain

Wisdom is applied knowledge.

I'm tired of straying off the path
just to come back
with more scars and more damage.

This life is not about the constant fixing.
It's about shifting and moving,
adapting and growing.

The constant healing has got to stop.
At some point, we have to take the knowledge
we've learned
and apply it to our life
so we can avoid the pain and suffering
that comes with straying off the path.

We have to be wise enough
to avoid the damage
and avoid the pain.

Deception

There is so much deception in this world,
and the thing about deception
is that it is always near to pride.

It's always fighting to prove a point
of who we are or what we're made of.
The deception is in the perception
that we have of ourselves.

I need to make lots of money so that
I can be respected.
I need to believe in this philosophy so that
I can look whole and put together.

The deception
is in all areas of our lives.
But it isn't until we lay down our pride
and say,

Actually, I don't know it all.
Actually, I'm just doing the best that I can.
And along that journey, I'm open to reason.
I'm open to ideas and ways of living
that I never really saw for myself
or had examples of.
I'm open
to the life that lies beyond
deception.

The why

Sometimes we think
we have to have it all together,
but the thing about life
is that it comes with uncharted weather.
When you have an understanding
of the *why,* you can figure out the *how*.

The *why*
isn't about figuring it out
but instead
building solid grounding for your mounting.
Build those roots that run deep.
Be solid in who you are
and where you want to go.
Know that wherever the wind blows,
you can find your way.
Your *why* is what gives you the reason
and direction.
Know that it will come together
in the best possible way.

Invitation

Your jealousy is not a reflection
of who you are;
your jealousy is a symptom
of what's in your heart.

What's in our hearts isn't always pure.
It's a reflection of our desires
and our ambitions.
It isn't that you're bad
for feeling jealous.
It's what you do with the jealousy
that counts.

Use it as a navigation system
to what it is you truly feel.
Use it as a traffic light
to what you consume.
Use it as an invitation
to call on something greater
and develop your faith and strength.

We allow symptoms to separate us from freedom
when really they are invitations.
To grow in faith and strength,
use them before they use you.

It's not luck

I don't believe in luck.
I don't think good things just happen.
I think we set ourselves up for what's to come.
And if we plant good seeds,
then we grow good trees.
If we put in the work,
then we reap the benefits,
and not always in the way
that we envision and plan
or even hope for.
But in a way that's silently fulfilling,
in a way that meets our needs
without feeding our greed.

I don't believe in luck.
I think we get what we give.
And yeah, bad things happen sometimes,
but even when they do,
they can always be turned around.
We can always make something good.
It just depends on how you perceive it.

Low moments

For some reason,
things always seem to take a turn
when we've hit a new low.
It's almost as if life is waiting for us
to look outside ourselves,
or maybe even inside ourselves.

"What got me here?" *ignorance*
"How was I so blind?" *naivete*
"Did I really just do that out of pride?" *confusion*

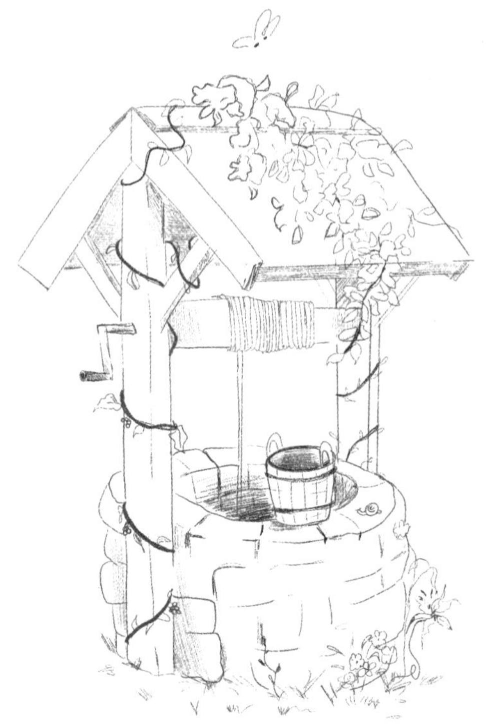

It's in our lowest moments
when we get a good look at ourselves.
We see how we've been moving
and how our ideas
were really just a way of getting by.
Of filling ourselves up
with what we thought we needed
or what we've been taught to need.

We've got to get low to that point
where our pride is left
with nothing by its side.
Because it's in those moments
when we get to decide.
We get to see ourselves.

The low moments
are an opportunity for redirection.
And although that may be scary
and intimidating, it's also exciting.

It's the start of something new.
You're heading down a path that is different,
that is brighter.

More to life

I promise you,
life is not about the things you acquire
or the places that you go.
I promise you,
life is more than the things
you have to show.

We get caught up in the day-to-day,
and it's fair to say
that sometimes
we lose our way.
We lose our way in the expectations
people have of us,
in the plans that we set.
But I want you to remember
that on your way,
there is joy and peace.
On your way,
there is time and patience.
On your way,
there is space to figure it all out.

It's not all about the things you have or do.
Life is more than what you are going through.

Spirit vs. flesh

You know when your spirit knows something,
but your body just hasn't caught up yet?
My spirit knows I'm going to do great things.
My spirit knows that I'm capable of so much more,
that I'm going to move on to bigger and better.
But my body hasn't caught up yet.

My body is still stuck in the pattern of overthinking.
My body is still stuck in the memories that haunt
me,
those rhymes and routines
that have been on repeat.

I'm aching for what feels good,
for what I enjoyed in the past.
Not knowing
that there is so much more waiting for me.
Not knowing
that on the other side of my discomfort is
the evolved me.
The new and improved me, the unrecognizable me.
The me that I always knew I would be.

Don't get discouraged.
Know that it's only a matter of time
until your body catches up with your spirit.
Until you do it
with ease.

Stumble

You've got to be humble enough to stumble.
You've got to be humble enough to recover.

If the expectation is perfection,
then you will always be disappointed.
Choke up, stumble, fall!
Whatever it is you do,
stop hiding it.

Allow yourself to be imperfect;
we all are.
It might not look the same on every
single one of us,
but we've all got flaws.
And we all have imperfections.
So if your standard
is to always be perfect
and put together,
man, are you doing yourself a disservice.
Man, are you putting on
the pressure of the world.

And for what?!
So people can see you in a brighter light?
So you can hide the things that we can all relate
to?
C'mon, you've got to find your confidence.
You've got to know that it's not that big of a deal
to fall or fail.

High

There's going to be a day
when it all makes sense.
There's going to be a day
when you don't need to get high
to get by.
There's going to be a time
when everything
is fine.
When your fears are cast away.
When you can breathe
a little lighter.
When your laughter feels so real
that nothing else
really matters.

There's going to be a time
when you look back
and wonder,
"Why did I ever think that this was it?
Why did I ever think that it was over?"

There's going to be a time,
because you are going to make it
through this time.

Heart sounds

I still hear your heart.
We get stuck in anger and resentment,
then end up frustrated
because we can't hear their heart.

Although it's not our responsibility
to hear the cries of others
and meet the needs that they have,
it does the world and our own lives a service
to simply listen to the cries of their hearts.

We are all connected in our humanness.
We're all crying out to be loved or seen,
to be heard or understood.
The quicker we can get to the space
of understanding the heart,
the faster we can let go of resentment
and understand what lies beneath.

We can connect in our cries
and move into a space of acceptance.
Move into a space of forgiveness.
Listen beyond what you can see or perceive
to the cries of their heart.
To the cries
of what they truly need.

Curious soul

Discernment is the ability to judge well. Sometimes we see a door open and automatically think that, because it's open, it's for us to walk through. But not every door that opens is meant for us. This is where discernment comes in, where we need to challenge our curiosity and the intrigue that makes us wonder and question, then go seek in every direction. With discernment, you can question, then learn by being patient in what you don't know. It's learning through listening to others and asking the right questions, then developing understanding over time.

Afraid to heal

I'm kind of embarrassed to say this,
but if I'm being honest,
if I'm being really real,

I'm afraid to heal.

I'm afraid to heal and end up in the same place.
I'm afraid to move past what I think I've
overcome,
past what I think I've learned,
just to end up in a similar situation.
Because how many times have we learned
and put on new ways
just to find out that underneath it
is still pain?
Underneath it
is still insecurity.

We say,

"I no longer get angry.
I know how to calm myself down."
But underneath is still anger and frustration.

"I'm no longer stressing over the little things."
But underneath is a worrisome mind.

I'm afraid to heal
not because I don't think that it's real,
but because **I'm afraid of putting on**
when I should be taking off.

Projector

We all want the same things;
we just go about getting them
in different ways.

Some of us want to be heard,
so we scream and shout
in fits of anger
with hopes that we can be seen
through our volume.

Some of us want to be felt
and accepted,
so we spread ourselves thin.
Giving a piece of who we are
to everyone who comes by,
to anyone who shows a bit of attention.

We try to fill ourselves
with the false sense of closeness
that company brings.
But until we understand
that our counterproductive
and self-destructive ways
are getting in the way of us finding our way,
we'll continue to wear the mask
of our persona.
We'll continue to seek out
what we want
in ways that lead us astray.

Instead of bleeding out
and hiding what it is we feel,
let's be brave enough to look deeper.
Let's be brave enough
to heal the wounds within.

Support

Oftentimes, we judge other people
as hard as we judge ourselves.
It's commonly said that if you aren't creating,
then you're critiquing,
and it's true.
The more you focus on yourself,
the less you can focus on others.
The more you focus on you,
the more you realize
just how far support
can go, just how far
a word of encouragement
can truly help you grow.

If you're worried about criticism,
remember that the ones criticizing
are probably not doing much realizing.
Don't let it hold you back.
Look at other people
and start to encourage them.
Be the support you think
you need.

Judging heart

A judging person has a judging heart,
and a judging heart doesn't have eyes.
Your judgment is not selective.
It doesn't pick and choose who to abuse
with comments and quick remarks.
A judging heart judges everyone
and everything.

You think it doesn't include you,
but think again. A judging heart
is equipped with habits and routines.
The way you pick apart others
is also how you'll pick apart yourself.

Before you judge anyone,
ask yourself if you can take the heat.
If you were put in their shoes,
could you take it how you dish it?

It's time we start to treat others
how we want to be treated.
It's time you start to look at others
how you would look at yourself.

Bigger than you

We all have our uniqueness.
We all have the urge to be totally
and unapologetically free.
It isn't unique to feel that,
but how we express that
is unique.

How our desires come into fruition,
how they come to the surface,
is unique.
Some of us have more control
or the ability to filter
what we think and feel.
And how we choose
to express ourselves
is a reflection of our filter.
Should we change that filter?
Should we get rid of that filter?

That's up to you.
But I will say that sometimes
that filter gets junky.
Sometimes that filter
needs to be renewed,
and a change is due.

Take care of yours.
Make sure your filter isn't stopping you
from being and doing
what God has called
of you.
Your life
is bigger than you.

Speak up

If something doesn't feel right,
if you are uncomfortable,
speak up.

A lot of times, we put ourselves through
uncomfortable
and even somewhat dangerous situations
because we're afraid to speak up.
We're afraid of the reaction we'll get.

"If I say that I'm uncomfortable,
will they think that I'm needy?
"Does how I feel in this situation really matter?"

The answer is yes!
A million times over, **yes!**
Your voice is powerful.
As small or insecure,
as unsure as you feel in any situation,
speak up.

Speak up for yourself because,
as harsh as it sounds,
it's your responsibility to protect your mind
and your body.
If you don't stand up for yourself,
no one else will.
And not because no one cares
but because not everybody knows
when you need to be stood up for.

Use your voice and say how you feel.
Speak up for yourself
and know that **what you feel is real.**

RESILIENCE

Letter to myself

Stop trying to get back to the old you;
she doesn't exist anymore.
What you've been through,
what you've experienced,
has changed you.
You're different now.
You're wiser, you're smarter,
you understand people differently now.
Your worldview has changed.
Different things excite you now,
like expanding your creativity
and connecting with God.
Expressing yourself out loud is freeing now.
You are not the same person anymore.
You've changed and you've grown.
You are a whole new you,
and it's time you start to accept her.
Trust me, she's supercool.

The journey

Your journey will be unique.
Your journey will not look like any other.
It is a journey one must take with a willingness
to find truths within the truths.

There will be twists,
and there will be turns.
And along that path
you will find gems and stones
of wisdom
that bring you closer
into alignment.

This journey is all-encompassing.
It considers all aspects
of the mind, body, and soul.
It is one that requires fearless ambition.
The journey will make up
the story of your life.

I am not the standard

I am not the standard.
What works for me
is what works for me,
and what works for you
is what works for you.

When you make yourself the standard,
you start to miss out
on what it truly means
to love and accept.

It is not my job
to push and press
what I see as valuable,
what I see as better,
onto the people around me.
Sometimes we forget
what love really is.
We forget that love
is a choice.
When it comes to the people around you—
your friends, your family,
the people who are close to you—
the best way to love
is by giving them the freedom
to come as they are.

Not everyone has the standard
that you have.
Not everyone has the goals
that you do.
But what a shame

to let that blind you.
What a shame
to let that block you.

Accept people
for who they are
and how they want to live.
And through that,
your love will be felt.
Through that,
your love will be shown
and received.

Stop making yourself
the standard.

Give it time

You will never know
how something is supposed to play out
until you let it play out.
It sounds so simple
and so clear,
but for some reason,
we get caught up in wanting to know
everything.

But remember that you have made
good decisions before.
Remember that it played out in your favor,
even when you had no idea that it would,
and when it didn't,
you always found your way back.

There is nothing to fear.
There is nothing to run away from.
Check your heart, check your gut and your intuition;
sometimes they'll lead you astray.
Pray about it, talk about it
with your friends and with your people.
Give it what it needs.
Give it
time.

Abundantly joyful

It all flows from joy.
Know that when the bad times pass,
the good times follow.
That there is so much goodness
that flows from the abundant
space of joy.

It's the joy and the gratitude for life
that allows us to walk into rooms
with confidence,
knowing that *what is or isn't for me*
can never miss me.
Knowing that *I am eternally guided and protected,*
and that as much as my future is in my hands,
it is ultimately
in the hands of God.

I am guided,
I am protected,
and I am grateful
through it all.

There's no rush

I feel like there's so much on my plate.
There's always the weight
of what could be
or what should be.

I feel like there's no time to waste,
like if I stay in one place,
I'll be late.

But as I sit and start to enjoy
the sweet little moments
of nothingness,
I realize that there was nothing to rush.
There was nothing passing me by.

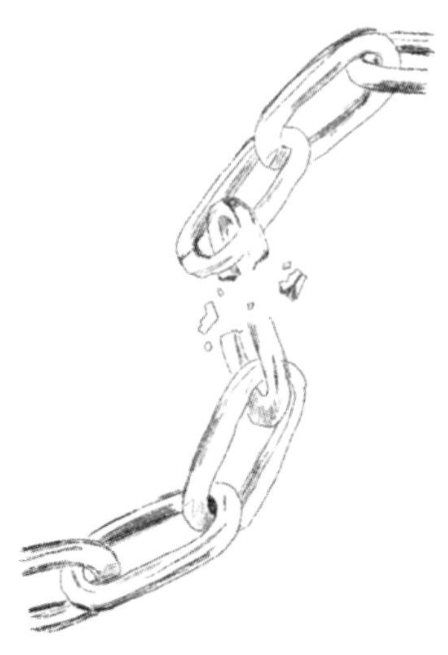

It was fear.
It was my fear that told me where to go
and how to do it.
But this time around,
I'm not falling through it.

I'm not letting the thorns of my mind
choke what could be mine.
I'm not suffocating the time that I have
with the distance I create
from what genuinely fills my spirit.

I'm not selling myself short.
For my fear, for whatever it is I see
in that rearview mirror.

I'm not looking back.
My future is in front,
so I have to run.

Run at a pace that is true,
run at a pace that is filled
with faith and love
and guidance
from You.

Bright futures

The power of presence
comes from understanding
that the *now* is creating your future.
You have no idea who you are becoming.
Soaking up every moment
and living life in the present
is what allows us to fill our future.

The focus shifts from anticipating everything
that is to come
to soaking up everything that *is, right now.*
Everything that truly fills your spirit.

With that comes gratitude,
for all that you have
and all that you don't.
And an ease over your anxiety.
It's what carries us through
into a brighter future.

Now what?

Where do I go
when I've done what I set out to do?
Where do I go
when everything I achieve
never seems to relieve
my wandering curiosity
for where I'm supposed to be?

What should I do?
When I continuously ache
to try something new,
to find new views and heights
that make me feel new,
what do I do?

When I feel called to something great
but can never stay in one place.
Maybe that's what it is:
Stay in one place.
Stay in the present;
allow it to do what it does.
Stay in one place;
be great in this place.

Allow your wandering spirit
to feel the space.
Stay
in one place.

Be still

Be still.
When you feel like the world is running
at a million miles per hour,
be still.
When you feel like your mind
is racing through confusion and doubt,
trying to figure out
how the future will play out,
be still.
The answers don't come from overthinking;
they come from a surrendering spirit.
The only way to peek into the future,
the only way to find clarity,
is simply by being present.

I want to know if I made the right decision.
I want to know if I'm doing what I'm supposed to do.

Then keep doing it.
Keep doing it with faith and hope.
Keep doing it with stillness.
Don't get caught up in the he said, she said.
Don't even get caught up in your own thoughts.
Keep moving forward in stillness
and in silence.

Here

Being at peace with your future is really about finding your focus, and a way that you can do that is by totally immersing yourself in the present moment. How many of us have goals and ambitions that we want to achieve? Aside from the skills you need to learn, you probably also have a timeline. Although this is wonderful and even essential for success, it's also important to remain focused on the present. Focus calls for our attention, so if in the moment you let your focus drift toward the future, you also let it drift toward the uncertain. If our attention is on what's uncertain, we're bound to feel anxious. Allow yourself time to rest and focus on what you find in the present moment. It's in the present moment that you fill yourself with everything you need to achieve your future goals.

Under mind

To all the people who are doubting themselves
and questioning their own worth:
Is it not a little suspicious that the second you boss up
and find yourself, you also start to shine?

Is it not a little weird that underneath all the noise,
underneath the lies,
is a flower that's already bloomed?

A lot of times, the noise we hear in our mind,
the voice that tells us we're not good enough
or it's too much work,
is the very same voice
that feeds us the lie of who we are not.

Is it not funny how the fear and anxiety
of an outcome
that hasn't even happened
is what holds us back?
What keeps us stagnant in the same place for ages?

I'm calling out all those lies.
I'm telling you
that the person beneath the noise
is louder.
The person beneath the noise
has already bloomed.
Now it's up to you
to dig in and see what you find
underneath your mind.
I guarantee you'll find something great.
I guarantee you'll find something
that you already knew.

Smoke and mirrors

It's really just smoke and mirrors.
What you see in others
also exists within yourself.
You are capable;
you just haven't put yourself out there.
You haven't let yourself fall a couple times
to know that you can get up.
You already have it within you.
The ability is already there.

Go out and be brave.
Go toward that humbling force that clears the air,
that shows you exactly who you are
and what you are capable of.
Don't let the smoke cloud your vision.
Don't let the mirrors throw you off.
Know who you are and know what you can do.
Start to move straight through.

Just be you

If you were just you,
if you didn't do your hair in a trendy way
or wear the clothes you thought other people
wanted to see you in,
you would be so attractive.
You would literally shine!

But you think you have to cover who you are
to be accepted.
You think that the layers add to who you are,
but really, they just take away.
They're taking away from your essence,
they're taking away from the thing
that makes you *you*.

You have to be brave.
You have to stop caring what other people think.
Underneath all of that
is the you who is going to shine.
Oh my goodness!
You are going to shine!
And you are going to light up the whole room!
Just be you.

Something big

Don't get discouraged
by what you think you have.
Don't get discouraged
by what you think you lack.
It's a very real thing to walk into a room
and feel unworthy,
but in those places and times,
you must remember
that who you are
is not who you are becoming.

There will always be someone
who is better than you,
who has put in more time,
who has more experience and skills.
But you cannot let that stop you from becoming
the best version of yourself.
Sometimes we never reach our best
because we're afraid to start
from the bottom.

Forget about what you think people think,
forget about their opinions,
and start creating and living
in a way that is best
for you.
That is aligned for you.

Don't allow anything
to keep you small.
Being small
is the start
of something big.

The magic

The magic happens when you start.
The magic happens
when you decide to embark
on the journey
rather than thinking about all the reasons
why it would never work out.

Once you get into the motions of it,
once you physically start doing
what you're supposed to do,
the mind follows.
And the mind follows with positivity,
with endless faith
and a willingness
to overcome challenges.
Once you have the mind
and body working together,
God comes in
and takes it to another level.

Space

There's space for you.
In the field you want to get into,
in the career, the business, the passion,
whatever it is.
There is not only a space for you,
but there is a spot
waiting for you.

You've got to understand that what you bring
is **unique.**
Your **perspective** is unique.
Your **delivery** is unique.
Your **passion** and **focus**
are unique.
What you bring will always be different
regardless of how saturated the field is.
Bring what you've got to the table,
walk in with confidence,
and trust that what you bring
is valuable, because it is.

Just show up

It's time we start doing the things
that we were meant to do.
It's not a matter of changing your habits
and being disciplined to become
someone new.

You don't have to be afraid;
you are already good enough.
And you don't have to worry,
because it's already within you.
All you need to do is show up.
All you need to do is allow it
to flow from you.

Muzzled

I'm about to walk into my confidence.
Yes, I did say what I said,
and you know why?
I said it because I meant it.
I said it because this is where I am at.

I don't owe you an apology
or an explanation.
I can simply be.
I'm allowed to be me.
If it sits right with me,
then I'm going to let it be.

I am done with the coddling,
with the constant checking in,
with the overexplaining.
It's draining.
This is me,
and this is how I'm showing up.
If there's conflict, we can resolve it.
If you're offended, we can talk.
But I am done muzzling myself
for the sake of your
comfort.

You against you

You are on your own race;
it's you against you.
It's not you against everyone else.
It's not even you against the timeline
you set out.
You have to show up
and put your best foot forward
until **you** feel it's enough.
You have to be the best that you can be
until **you** feel satisfied.
It's never about other people
and what they think or what they have.
It's about you.
It's about you and how you feel about you.
Are you happy with how you show up?
Are you happy with what you've done?
It's never about other people;
it's about you.

Made for you

You know the best thing you can do
is focus on you.
Don't look at others
and compare what they have.
Focus on you and what you are working through.
A lot of times, we compare ourselves
to what we think people have,
who we think people are.
Without even realizing
that your life
and your journey
are just as complex.

Instead of focusing
on the other side,
start to water what's on yours.
Start to water the things that fill you.
Start to become that person
that you're proud of.
Because I guarantee
that a life of comparison will do nothing
but continuously put you down
off of a basis that isn't even real.

Know that your life is just as great.
It doesn't look or sound the same
as anyone else's,
but it's great,
and it's good,
and it was made for you
to work through.

Work through it

Long story short,
don't try and fight your shortcomings,
just work through them.

Everything happens for a reason.
Every struggle, every challenge you face
is for a reason.
Sometimes we have flaws or quirks
that aren't the greatest.
Sometimes we struggle through things
that others easefully walk through.
But don't ever think, even for second,
that your struggle makes you less than.
It's not to say that we should accept the things
we struggle with,
that we should wear them as a part of our
identity,
no.
Your struggle is unique to you,
and it will resolve into something
unique too.

Don't try and fight it.
Don't try and remove it,
just work through it.

Feeling stuck

What God has for you
will never miss you.
What you were meant to do in this world
can never miss you.
What you were called to do
has always been calling you.

They can think it's weird,
and they can say it's not you,
but only you and God
know the plans that He has for you.
The vision you have
was given specifically to you.
It wasn't given to your friends,
it wasn't given to the people
looking from the outside in;
it was given to you.

And because it was given to you,
it's now your responsibility
to execute.
It doesn't matter what everyone else thinks.
They do not have the full picture.
You do.

Rubble

Know that there is value in the rubble.
Know that even in your time of distress,
even when you feel worthless,
there's a silver lining, and it is worth it.

Your life is not a burden.
You feel things deeply,
and you feel it because it's real.
Your hurt is real,
but it is not all
that there is.

When you are in the rubble,
it only makes sense for it to be cloudy.
It only makes sense for you to not be able
to see things through.

But even in the rubble,
you are worthy;
even in the rubble,
your life has purpose.
Keep pushing forward,
because this does not define you.

Fantasy

You know, reality isn't so bad
once you've accepted it.
A lot of us get frustrated
and triggered with the little things in life
because, well, our reality doesn't match
our fantasy.
When the little things aren't perfect, we're triggered.
When you face an inconvenience, you're angered,
and when you feel like the obvious
isn't so obvious to everyone else,
you're annoyed.

These are all symptoms
of being frustrated with reality.
We get stuck in the present moment
where we feel like our current reality
is our destiny.

But where you are now
is not where you will be forever.
The struggles you face
will progress as you do.
As soon as you accept your reality,
you also accept the opportunity
to move in a direction that's fitting.
Keep your head held high
and don't allow the little things
to get to you.
This right here
is not your forever.

Do better

You could have all the ideas in the world,
but if you aren't able to make the moves,
what's the use?
Sometimes it isn't about what you know,
but instead
how you use the information.
If you're at a place where you finally know better,
where you've lived and learned
and feel like you can start to do better,
it's time you start to put that knowledge
into action.

And I know it's scary,
because it means that there is change.
It means that what you know
is no longer solid.
But I want you to remember
that you are smart,
that the ideas you have
are solid.
That they have potential.
It's up to you to bring them to fruition.
You've got to be the driving force.
You know better,
but now it's time
for you to do better.

New start

It's in the dark moments when God is near.
It's in the moments when everything is crashing down
and it feels like you're hitting rock bottom
that you actually get to see
what wasn't working.

You become aware
of how your foundation
wasn't firm enough to hold.

So don't be afraid,
don't even worry:
God is near to the brokenhearted.
God is near to the ones
that see their destruction
and realize that it wasn't the way.

If you are in a place
that feels like rock bottom,
if you are in a place
that feels like it's being destroyed,
remember that this is your opportunity.

This is your opportunity to build something new,
to build a foundation that can weather the storm.
I know you feel down,
I know you feel like the world is over,
but this is the beginning of a fresh start.

Stepping over

You're trying to bring other people down,
not realizing
that you don't even stand
on solid ground.
What good is it
to bring other people down
so you can feel up?
What good does it bring
to hide what truly hurts,
refusing to admit
where you actually feel small?

The longer you refuse to look at yourself
and see what actually hurts,
the longer you will suffer.
The more you look at everyone else
and use their shortcomings
to validate your insecurities,
the longer you will be stuck.
Because there is no moving through
without going through.
You cannot move through
by stepping on other people's backs
to heal from what you lack.
You cannot heal
by filling your ego and sense of self.
You have to admit where you feel small.
You have to be humble enough to do so.

I know it's hard, and I know it hurts,
but this is where it starts.

You're good now

You're good now,
but don't let go.
Don't let go of the beauty that was shown
in the garden that was grown
on your pain.
You're good now,
but remember the rain.
The rain that cleared your vision,
that showed you more
than what you could see before.
You learned
that your body isn't up for sale,
that it isn't on display
for anyone to say
or have their way.
Your beauty
is so much more than any compliment could give.
Your value
needs to be protected.

You're good now,
but the lessons still remain.
You're free now,
and the pain wasn't in vain.
Don't go back to what you used to do.
Don't go back to what you're used to.
Remember your pain,
and please,
please remember
to stay in this new lane.

Nothing new under the sun

There is nothing
I am currently going through
that someone else
hasn't already been through.
I know that I am not alone in the things that I face,
that what I am going through
has a solution.
I know that I'm unique, but my challenges
are not unique to me.
I'm under the sun;
all of this has been done.

Take control

At some point
you've gotta take the ball
back into your court,
because to move on
and truly let it go,
you have to take control.
You have to take accountability
for the decisions you made
and the vulnerability that you gave.

And it's not to say
that you did anything wrong;
it's not to say
that it's all your fault.
But it is to say
that you must start writing
the rest of this narrative.
Because if you don't,
this experience will write all over you,
and if you don't,
this hurt will bleed
all over what is true.

So yes, it happened.
And yes, it broke a piece of you,
but what is in the works
is a rebuilding of something new.
What is in the works
is greater than that old you.

Pain is temporary, and experiences
come and go,
but how they shape you
is in your control.

Alchemist

I don't need a perfect life.
I can turn anything into art.

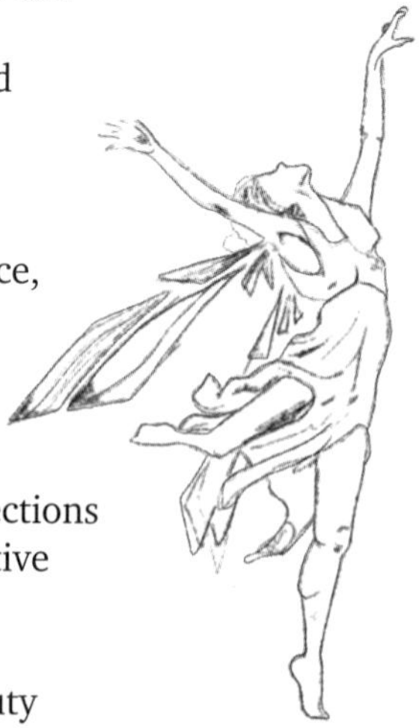

I have everything I need
to make and turn
what I need
into what I have.
The big and grand is nice,
but what I have
will suffice.
I see beauty
in everything I touch.
I know that the imperfections
are what bring perspective
and understanding.

Just like me, I find beauty
in the things that don't always make sense,
in the things that hurt but tell a story.
I know that every situation
has potential
to be turned and flipped,
to be made anew.
I find beauty
in anything
and make it
into something.

Forget it

Forgive and forget,
but carry the lessons with you.
Understand that the knowledge
is separate from the teacher.
The teacher is the one who hurt you;
the lesson is the knowledge that they taught you.

Yes, they hurt you and left you scarred,
but take that knowledge and apply it,
to them and everyone else.
You might have to put up those boundaries.
You might even have to learn some self-control.
But understand that the teacher
can always grow.
The teacher can evolve.
The lesson, on the other hand,
is what remains the same.

Forget about what they did.
You have the knowledge now;
go and apply it.

Power of forgetting

I say forgive and forget:
Forget what that person did to you,
but don't forget the lessons they taught you.

When you forget, you let go of the past.
When you forget, you integrate the experience
you had with the lessons you learned.
You come to an understanding
that the grudge has no purpose.

Don't give people the power to control you.
Don't give them more than what's due.
Forget about it, forget what they did;
it doesn't control you.
That lesson, that overarching lesson,
is what stays with you,
not them.

Mental strength

The more I live,
the more I learn
that, within every turn,
there is something to learn.
A strong mind is a strong life.
It's within our minds
that we create our external world.
It's within our minds
that we build a world
that can not only survive the realities
but bring back the subtleties.

"I thought I was good then,
but look how great I'm about to get."

It's within my perceived failure
that I get to redeem myself,
that I get to prove myself right.
Start to build that mental strength,
start planting those seeds
of positivity and hope and optimism.
Remember to water them well
with grace and patience.

A humble spirit

A humble spirit can conquer
anything.
It's within our humility
that we find the space to grow
and expand what we already know.

There's something about
a humble spirit
and its willingness to get low.
There is no image to keep up.
There is no facade to portray.
A humble spirit is willing
to do whatever it takes
in order to grow.
Whether it's a season of serving
or a season of lying low,
a humble spirit
knows it's role.

It doesn't allow the outside noise
to take a toll;
it's already low.
The only place for it to go
is up, the only place for it to go
is in the direction
of growth.

Empty

Not trusting God
pulls you further away from Him.
Not trusting God replaces His plan
with yours.
You wonder why you get in phases
of depression and loneliness.
You wonder why it feels like nothing is worth it.
The plan that just keeps nagging you?
The lack of fulfillment that's grabbing you?
That is God trying to speak to you.
It's a good thing you're feeling unfulfilled.
It's a good thing you're feeling uncomfortable.
Don't get down and out over where you are:
God is still with you.

Where you start is not where you finish

We can't grow unless we steward.
To steward is to make the best out of what you already have;
it's taking care of what you've been given.
Through that comes growth.
Through that comes wisdom and knowledge.
Focus on where you are.

Remember that everything has a starting point,
but where you start is not where you finish.

Good steward

Remember to focus
on the task at hand;
remember that your focus
and efficiency are fueled
not by your productivity
but instead
by accepting the responsibility
to steward and to care
while we wait for
what has always been
in store.
It's not about the amount of things
we can do within an hour
but how we water
each flower.
Focus on the task at hand
and know that what is to come
has already
been planned.

Take a break

Let's take a beat.
Let's relax,
learn how to breathe.

Let's take in the moment.
Let's turn every frown
upside down.
Let's wear our joy
rightfully so.

Let's take a beat.
Let's soak our feet
in something neat,
in what sparks our interest
and brings us peace.

Let's relax,
learn how to breathe.
Inhale the beauty
and exhale
all of its forms.

Let's fill the world
with our bright ideas.
Let's soothe it with our spirit.

Let's learn
how to just be.

Different

Trust yourself.
Trust that you made the right decision.
Trust that standing firm
on your morals and beliefs
will make sense in time.

Remember that you are here for a reason,
remember that whatever shift or turn
is happening in your life,
God is still with you.
God is still here.

Sometimes we get sad over the fact
that our lives no longer look the same,
our lives are looking
a little different this season.

Maybe it's a little quieter;
maybe you're in a season
where your focus has shifted
and you're working on things
that you pushed aside for years.

Whatever it is,
your life feels different.
But different doesn't always mean bad.

Narratives

Sometimes we build connections
through the insecurities
we have.

You're afraid to be alone,
you think that it says something about you,
you think the lack of attention
is a reflection
of who you are.

You're afraid to get close.
You think that if you do,
you'll somehow lose
yourself and all that it means
to be you.

These fears are what pull us in
or push us away.
The narrative we tell ourselves
is what we seek to find.

You are lovable,
and the attention you crave
is okay.
Learn to manage those feelings
so they don't blind what you see
or relate to in others.
Find the courage
to give a little of what you have
so that you can build what you want.

The way we connect with others
is a reflection of the beliefs we have.
And so remember:
There is so much about you to love.
You don't have to fear what's to come;
have faith and know that everything will be okay.

Stop looking back

Stop looking back
trying to find confirmation and comfort.
You have everything you need to proceed.

It's new and unfamiliar;
of course you're going to want
what feels similar.
But you cannot let your past blind your future.
You cannot keep searching for what is lost.

Be brave enough to step forward,
be brave enough to have faith
that it will all be okay.

Heart

One thing we can all benefit from
is softening our hearts.
One thing we can all strive for
is compassion.
To understand that sometimes
our actions are a symptom
of the world around us,
that the way we cope
is a reflection of our hope,
and sometimes,
that hope just isn't there.

It's understanding
that everybody, including you,
is fighting a battle.
Whether you see the vines
that keep them confined
or are blind
to the struggles
of their day-to-day.
Know that we are all working through
and getting through
our own challenges.
Instead of leaning
on anger and frustration,
start to lean on compassion
and understanding.
I know it can be hard,
but your compassion
is really a reflection
of your hope.

Accountability

Nobody owes you anything,
so you better take all your hurt
and your pain
and turn it into the accountability
that you have
for your role.

Despite your situation,
and despite how things have played out,
two good things can never produce bad.
So before you cast judgment
and blame someone else for how you feel
and the pain that was caused,
ask yourself,
What role did I play?
Did I really act out of love?
Because love does not produce pain,
for yourself
or for others.
Did I really have the best intentions?
Or was it based on passion and excitement?
Was it rooted in the gratification of the moment?
It's hard to move past pain
unless you recognize the part that you played.
It's hard to make real change
unless you accept where you are
and the position of your heart.

Recognize it,
accept it,
and then go out and change it.

Making peace

Making peace with the past
is a task that can come in two ways:
accountability
and forgiveness.

Accountability for the role you played,
accountability for the pain that you caused,
because no coin is ever one-sided.
Every person in every situation
plays a role.
Be brave enough to take accountability
for yours.

Forgiveness is what we seek
when we've done wrong,
but in order to forgive others,
we have to forgive ourselves.
And in order to forgive ourselves,
we have to be humble.
Humble enough to see our faults,
humble enough to see
where we went wrong.
So be brave:
Be brave enough to see your true self,
and be brave enough to confront it.

Insecurities

I'm going to embrace it while I work on it.
I'm going to embrace the fact
that I don't have clear skin
while I work on clear skin.
I'm going to embrace the fact
that I get anxious
while I work on finding
my true sense of self and confidence.
I'm going to embrace the fact
that I have insecurities
while I work on them.
Because so often we let our insecurities
cripple us from the inside out.
We allow our insecurities
to keep us hidden; meanwhile, there is nothing
we can instantly change.

I know that there are things
that will make me feel better,
but while I work on them,
while I start to make those changes,
I'm also going to embrace where I am.
I'm not going to let my insecurity
keep me in hiding.

Confident

Be confident
without being cocky.
Assure yourself
in what you know to be true,
not what other people
say about you.

Lack of confidence

Your lack of confidence is not even real.
You are filled with so many talents and skills,
but you refuse to show them
because you're afraid of what others will think?
What about what you think?
I know that you know you're good;
I know that you know you are special
because when you're on your own
and you're doing your thing,
not only do you enjoy it
but it fuels you.
It lights something up within you.

Why would you think
that you are so
extraordinarily different
that no one else would enjoy
what you do?
If you feel something,
I guarantee you
there is someone out there
who feels it too.
Take your lack of confidence
and throw it somewhere far,
because you know who you are.
And you know
that you are special.

Forgive yourself

Don't forget to forgive yourself too.
Don't forget that everything
can be made new,
including you.
Don't forget that you are moving through,
that your past is a part of you
but was never meant
to keep you blue.
Don't forget that tomorrow
you can choose to be made new.
You can choose
something new to hold on to.
Don't forget that you are learning,
that you made mistakes
and you watched it fall through,
but that does not define you.
Start to walk through
what seems impossible.
Start to push forward;
start to persevere
through what seems
so unclear.
And watch how it starts to come together;
watch how it starts to flow
as you let go.

Confined

Sometimes we're afraid to let go
because we're afraid that nothing
better will ever come.
We're afraid that this is the end.
That where we are is as far as we'll ever go,
that it's all we'll ever have.
Little do we know
that our overthinking mind
is the only thing keeping us confined.
Underneath all those worries
and fears is the truth.
And the truth is that, as you let go,
you begin to receive.
As you make peace,
you begin to understand.
And as you take control,
you begin to see your role.
The role you played in the pain,
the role you had in the demise,
you start to see with different eyes.
And through it all
you begin to realize
that all you ever needed
to let go was to forgive.

Not the same

I wouldn't even wish on you
the way you made me feel;
that is forgiveness.
Forgiveness is deep surrender
to a situation that maybe you didn't have
control over
and still finding the space to say,
"Okay, I get that this really sucks right now,
but I am choosing to strive for better
and move toward the direction
of love."
Because what else is there?
What other option could favor
you, me, and everyone involved?
What other option
could be better than love?

Forgiveness is realizing
that the love you have to offer
is way more substantial
than the hate
and anger and envy
that you could hold on to.
The love you have within
ripples and spreads.
You must strive toward a direction
that is better.
Trust the principle,
trust the process,
and let it play out.

What is forgiveness?

Forgiveness is a call to understanding.
It's saying, I know that it wasn't your will
and intention to hurt me.
I know that you are working through
your own brokenness
and, through that process,
I was hurt.
I release any animosity toward you
and replace it with gratitude
for the times we spent in laughter and joy.
I pray you find your healing
and fill the void that causes you to hurt.
Forgiveness is letting go of their offenses
and understanding
that it was only a reflection
of their pain.
I forgive you,
as God has continuously
forgiven me.

Culture

Don't blame culture
for your lack of discipline.
Don't blame the media,
or even your lack of self-control,
on the culture that's being presented.
Your mind is your sanctuary;
it's yours to protect, and it's your responsibility
to keep it intact.
Life will continually come knocking on your door
with all sorts of lies
and hurts and struggles.
But that does not deny
that it is your responsibility
to turn and filter out those lies.
You have everything you need.
You are wise, and you are smart.
You are conscious, and you know
right from wrong—
even when you don't, your body tells you.
Listen and stop blaming everything else;
start looking at yourself.
You are in charge.

Out of focus

Focus on love;
watch how it heals and reveals.
Focus on you,
not what other people are up to,
not what other people
choose to do.
Focus
on what's right for you.
Get your direction right.
Stop bending and leaning on their path.
Stop spilling
all of what's inside you.
Be still,
be a reflection
so that others can find their direction.
Be open
to what others need.
Fill their cup up
and watch how yours spills over.
Give a little
and see how much is given to you.

Bird's-eye view

God is looking at your life
from a bird's-eye view.
He sees the challenges and the struggles
that you are going through.
He knows when you are at your wit's end
and feel like giving up.
He knows that there is so much beyond your
perseverance,
there is so much beyond that next try.
I know it's been a struggle
and it feels like all the pieces are scattered,
but maybe the scattered pieces
are what's putting it all together.
The scattered pieces
may be what's building you.
Have faith.
I know that you can do it,
and I know that you can persevere.

Real strength

I think sometimes, as women, we get so used to being on the defensive that we forget how to just be. We forget how to let a man take the lead and understand that that in itself is not living in defeat. That you have the choice to follow. That if where he is going isn't for you, you can leave. We think that being on the defensive is what keeps us safe, that wearing a shield of armor and fencing our hearts with standards is what keeps us safe, but it's not. It's knowing your worth and truly believing it; it's walking in your standards and not just putting up a fence until someone walks over it. You've got to know, and you've got to believe in your value. No standard can protect an unvalued prize, and no defense can keep out what you truly want in. You've got to know that you are more than what other people say or how they treat you. When you do that, you stop accepting less. Your strength isn't in your defense; it's in your confidence and belief of who you are.

Supposed to

Do what you're supposed to do
and watch how everything around you
starts to change.

Oftentimes, we know what we need to do—
we know what we need to change—
but we prolong it.
We put it off because we're afraid,
afraid of what is on the other side of our courage.

Will I be alone forever?
Will I look silly?
Is it even worth it?

These are the questions that run
through our minds
They are our worries and our fears
manifested into words and thoughts.
And the thing about our words and thoughts
is they become real things.
So every time you have a thought of doubt,
couple it with a thought of hope.

I might look silly at first, but
I will find my way, I will learn.
I might feel lonely at first, but
it will pass, I will find my people.

Task at hand

Oftentimes, we get stuck because
we haven't finished what's in front of us.
Instead of focusing
on all the things we have to do
and all of what's to come,
let's focus on what's here, right now.

What is here right now
that needs my focus and attention?
How can I show up
better and fuller
in this moment?
Do I need to take a break?
Do I need to take a breather?

Just for a second, forget about the future,
forget about what's to come, and focus
on what is here.

How can I make the best out of this situation?

Humbled

I'm definitely one of those people who believe that anything is possible. I truly believe that there is no dream and no challenge too big. But I've been humbled. I've been humbled by the fact that, although I have the capacity to overcome my challenges, those same challenges have the capacity to overcome me. I recognize the existence of my weakness. Within my strengths, I recognize my humanness, and it's actually within my humanness that I can proceed with the confidence to succeed. Because I also have the humility to fail and get back up again. I've been humbled. I've been humbled to the fact that I'm just as capable of succeeding as I am of failing. And it's actually been kind of freeing.

JOURNAL PROMPTS

Gratitude Practice

List three things that you are grateful for right now.

Why do you feel grateful for these things? Reflect on how each has impacted your life.

Explore a challenge you've faced recently. What did it teach you? How can you be grateful for the lessons you learned?

What are some ways you can express this gratitude and show appreciation for the gifts in your life?

Redefining Self-love

Explore the different ways self-love can extend beyond just caring for yourself.

How does your self-love empower you to serve others?

What does "self-love" mean to you?

What changes have you noticed in your relationships when you care for yourself?

Boundaries + Self-love
Think about the relationships you admire. What are some attributes a person must have for a relationship with you to truly thrive?

Reflect on how your boundaries are linked to your well-being (emotionally, physically, and spiritually).

How do you ensure your self-love doesn't fade when caring for others?

In what ways can you better communicate your boundaries?

Surrendering Control + Humility
What does it mean to "get low" so that God can lift you up?

Can you think of a time when you allowed God to take control? What were the results?

In what areas of your life do you struggle with pride? How might this be hindering you mentally and spiritually?

What are some signs you can recognize when pride is taking root in your heart?

Day-to-day
The magic of the mundane is in the reflection we find. When you look at your life in moments of quiet, is the reflection you see what you hope to mirror? Explore how you feel during the quieter seasons of your life.

How does the simplicity of your day-to-day life create space for reflection and growth?

How might embracing the ordinary days help you find clarity?

Challenging Limiting Beliefs
Sometimes our mind can tell us lies that we then start to believe. Write down some lies you've been telling yourself.

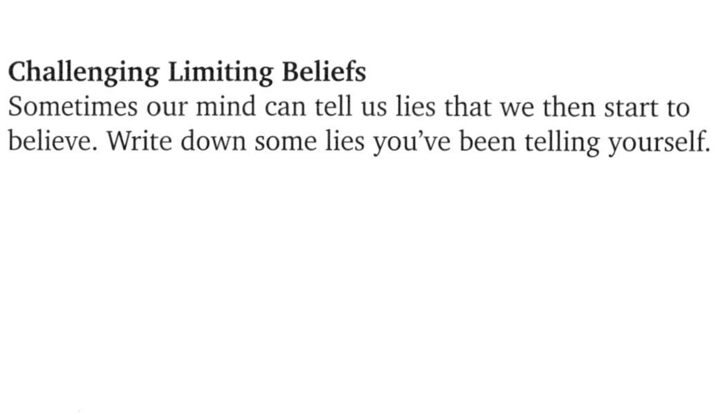

How have these lies held you back?

Now correct that lie with the truth. What are some things that are true about you?

Manifest
List three things you would like to manifest in your life.

How can you surrender these desires to God?

What does it look like to let go of control and trust that God will guide you toward the right path?

What does it mean to trust in God's goodness, even when things don't seem to be going your way?

How can you hold on to that trust when life gets difficult?

Mindset Shift

Think of something you would classify as a “mistake” you made. Why was it a mistake?

How has it shaped who you are today?

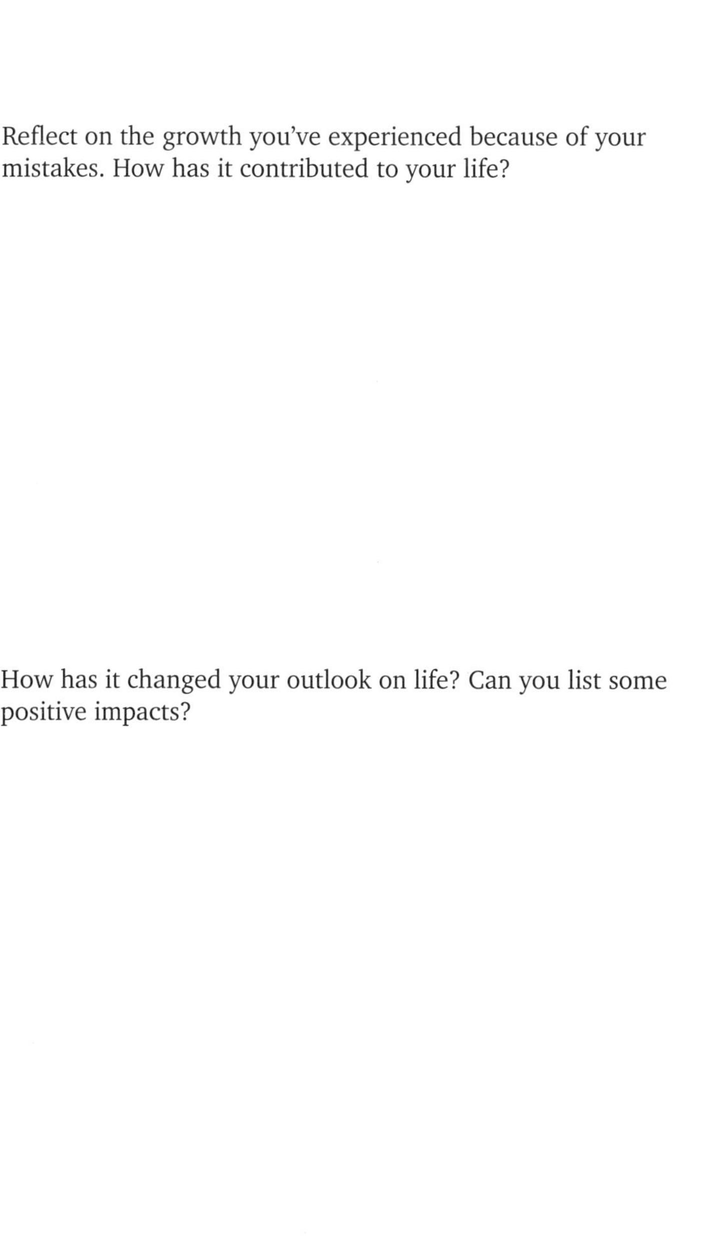

Reflect on the growth you've experienced because of your mistakes. How has it contributed to your life?

How has it changed your outlook on life? Can you list some positive impacts?

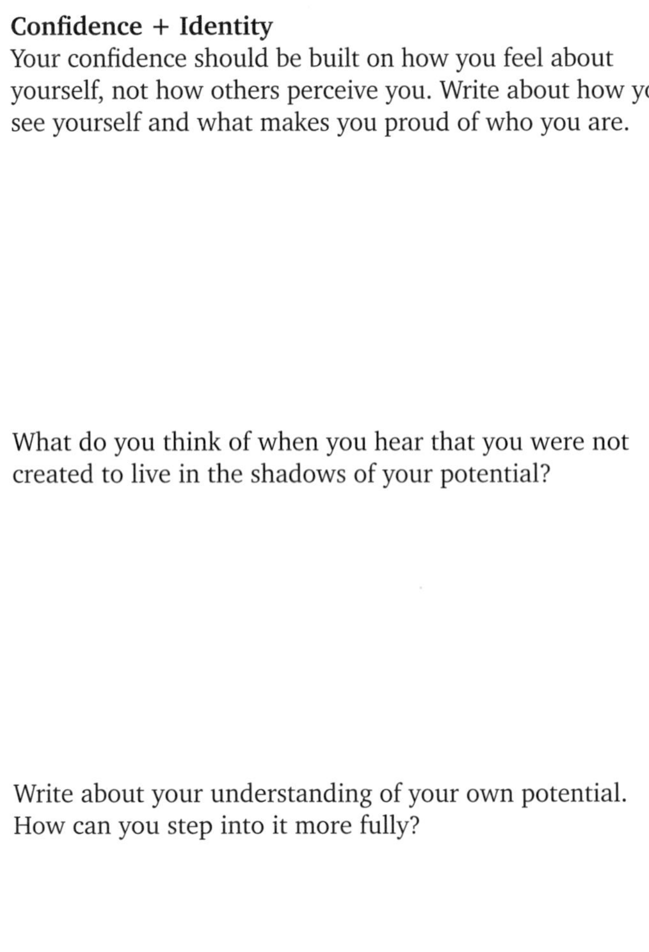

Confidence + Identity

Your confidence should be built on how you feel about yourself, not how others perceive you. Write about how you see yourself and what makes you proud of who you are.

What do you think of when you hear that you were not created to live in the shadows of your potential?

Write about your understanding of your own potential. How can you step into it more fully?

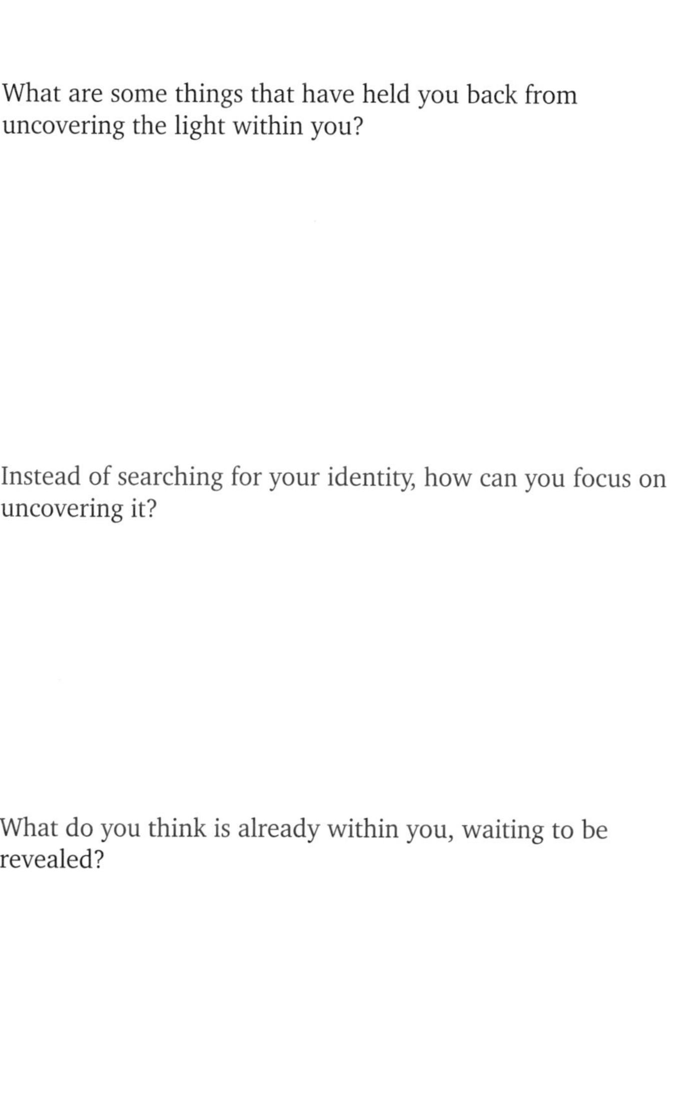

What are some things that have held you back from uncovering the light within you?

Instead of searching for your identity, how can you focus on uncovering it?

What do you think is already within you, waiting to be revealed?

Doing the Right Thing

Wisdom is applied knowledge. What are some lessons you've learned that you could start applying to your life right now?

Think about a cycle you've been stuck in. How can you break this cycle by actually applying what you've learned? What practical steps could you take?

What are some hard things you've been avoiding?

Why do you think they feel difficult, and what would happen if you decided to face them?

Growth + Change
In what ways have you changed over the past few years?

What aspects of this change do you appreciate or feel proud of?

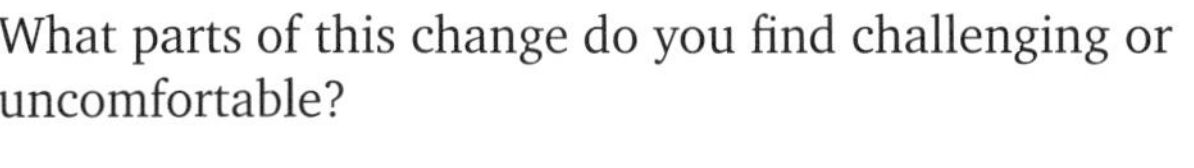

What parts of this change do you find challenging or uncomfortable?

You will never know how something is supposed to play out until you let it play out. What areas of your life require more time, patience, and trust?

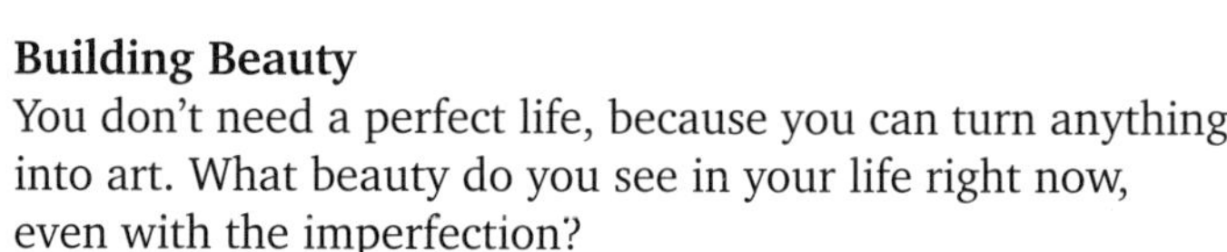

Building Beauty
You don't need a perfect life, because you can turn anything into art. What beauty do you see in your life right now, even with the imperfection?

Do you have any unique or unconventional perspectives on life? Write about one of them.

Love not only heals but also reveals. In what areas of your life can you focus more on love—whether in relationships, your work, or daily interactions?

About the Author

Abi Woldeab is a social media star who started writing by sharing her heart through video content. She acquired the admiration of thousands online and is said to be the "next voice in poetry" by *New York Times* bestselling author r.h. Sin. With a bachelor of science in nursing, Abi is not only passionate about caring for others in need but is inspired to encourage others throughout their journeys to find peace—physically, mentally, and spiritually. Her own personal journey through faith has led her to the profound truths that lie within her poetry. A language that is not only heard but deeply felt, her work offers new perspectives on the everyday challenges of life and mental health.

Abi is a first-generation Canadian from Eritrean descent currently living in Toronto, Canada.